My Spouse
My Friend

Ingiete Oyama

My Spouse My Friend
Copyright © 2020 by Ingiete Oyama

Tellwell Talent
www.tellwell.ca

ISBN
978-0-2288-4286-6 (Hardcover)
978-0-2288-4285-9 (Paperback)
978-0-2288-4287-3 (eBook)
978-0-2288-4887-5 (Audiobook)

Table of Contents

Dedication

This book is dedicated to the glory of the Almighty God and two very important men in my life, my father and my husband, who have been sources of courage and strength.

Acknowledgement

My greatest, deepest and heartfelt gratitude and thanks go to the Almighty God without whom this would not have been possible.

I want to thank my husband for his unshaken faith and support and my children for being my greatest inspiration, critics and support.

To my sweet mother and father who raised me and taught me the sky is not my limit but just a launching pad. I thank them for their wise counsel, for instilling faith in the Lord, discipline, courage, self-love, strength, and for making me understand that I had a purpose in life.

Special thanks go to my siblings who always loved and prayed for my success.

I want to thank everyone who contributed in one way or the other towards making sure this book was finally written and in print.

May the Lord bless and keep you all.

Introduction

The idea for this book resulted from having been married quite early in life and witnessing marriages coming under attack from the devil with couples giving up on each other even before the fight began. Marriages, or should I say spouses, like everything in our world, have become disposable! My spouse is geared toward revealing a brighter side of marriage, where it is fun and loving as God intended it to be.

However, it is my desire and prayer that as you progress through this book, couples would become more intentional in being friends and loving each other. They would fight for their marriages, homes and their children. I am convinced that the Lord God, who put this idea in me, would bless everyone with a very fulfilled marriage and God's blessings and protection. Hopefully, this book succeeds in bringing back the fun in marriage, where couples can be themselves and are not afraid to laugh freely with each other, and reinstates friendship, abundant love, and understanding between all couples. This book is where the lightheartedness of friendship and love exists, and where man and woman work toward the common goals of unity, happiness, and love.

My spouse, my friend!

The LORD God said, "It is not good for the man to be alone. I will make a helper suitable for him.

—Genesis 2:18

Chapter One

Mmmm, Marriage!

This word *marriage* evokes great joy in some and trepidation in others. What really is the definition of the word?

The word *marriage*, when used in any context, denotes a merger or union of two entities or bodies. However, *marriage* is defined as "the legally or formally recognized union of a man and a woman, typically as recognized by law, by which they become husband and wife" (the *Oxford English Dictionary*).

Marriage was God's perfect plan for the perfect union and, according to the Bible, is a union whereby a man leaves his father and mother and lives together with his wife and the two become one. This is seen in Genesis 2:24: "That is why a man leaves his father and mother and is united to his wife, and they become one flesh."

When we talk about marriage, the first thought that comes to mind is that it is a union between two people that is intended to create or lead to some intimacy wherein the two become one. It transcends any other human relationship and becomes a union that when formed according to the precepts laid down by God is rich, fulfilling, blissful, and blessed. The first marriage to take place on the face of the earth was in the Garden of Eden, as described in the Bible between Adam and Eve and witnessed by God Almighty.

Marriage involves much more than the partners taking a solemn vow before a minister and some witnesses. It is not about how large the crowd is, the pomp and pageantry that goes with it nor the size of the ring that adorns the fingers. We must not forget that marriage is witnessed by the Almighty God who first presided over marriage. It is a promise made by both partners to each other, in the presence of God, family, and friends. It reflects their integrity and a determination to be united in a sacred bond and then be the best they can be; first before God for each other, their families, and then the children when they make their appearance on the scene.

This sacred bond unites two people and makes them one. Ultimately, it also unites two families that ordinarily would have never coexisted: the beauty of it all is that this bond between man and woman has been established and ordained by God. The Bible records that the first marriage was instituted and solemnized by God in the Garden of Eden, where God made a decision and proceeded to create a helpmeet from

Adam's ribs. We will talk about this in a later chapter. This was done so that man's need for companionship, comfort, intimacy, and fulfillment could be met, as we see clearly in the Bible that "God thought that it is not good for man to be alone" (Genesis 2:18). This is a very powerful thought! Before man could even understand his physical and emotional needs, tend the garden, live his life, fulfill his responsibilities, and above all discover his need for companionship, God in His infinite wisdom knew that it was not going to be right for man to live alone! He had created animals and other creatures and living things on Earth, but these were not to be soulmates nor companions for man. Man needed his kind, someone he could relate to on the same plane, someone who would understand him, and he would do the same for; both would be in tune with each other and live a life worthy of their calling. They would lift each other up when they fell and be a source of strength for each other and even tolerate one another's excesses! This relationship was meant to be to the glory of God. This bond would glorify the Almighty God, that He would be at the centre of this bond intervening whenever He was called upon for help. The children born of this union would be brought up in the fear and love of the Lord, resulting in the birth of society.

It was a bond intended to be between man and woman. This bond was meant to bring two people from diverse backgrounds who are totally different in temperament, upbringing, sometimes cultures, and orientation together. It was meant to unite just two people, not three or four. If the reverse were to be the case, I am very sure God, who is all-powerful and all-knowing, would have made use of Adam's other ribs to create more women for him; after all, he still had a lot of them left for this purpose if He was so determined! I am sure that would have removed all confusion and given Adam free access to sampling the many women available at his disposal. Do I sense some skeptical expressions here? Well, "God is not a God of disorder but of peace..." (1 Corinthians 14:33, NIV). He knew that doing this would only result in dissatisfaction, chaos, jealousy, and a lack of contentment! Rather, He fashioned it in a way that these two individuals, joined together with a common purpose, would meet each other's needs; it was not intended that this bond be turned into a battlefield nor a competition of sorts geared toward establishing who is better than the other. Neither was it meant to become a battlefield for our egos.

God's intention behind the institution of marriage was to create companions who would meet each other at their point of need, lift each other up when the need arose, and complement the weaker partner with their strength. Made to complement one another in their different roles as husband and wife, God intended for the couples to work, live, and grow in harmony as a team. This was because working together as husbands and wives can accomplish way more than they could ever imagine when working individually. We can see this unity displayed by Aquila and Priscilla, who worked together as tentmakers (Acts 18:2–3) and were so dedicated to serving God and the people. They travelled together with Paul, ministered and brought people to the Lord. They even opened their home to the congregation; there was no sneaking around each other. They did it with all joy; there was no war of the sexes here! They were even commended by Paul in Romans 16:3–4 as he wrote glowingly about them thus: "Greet Priscilla and Aquila my co-workers in Christ Jesus. They risked their life for me. Not only I but the Churches of the Gentiles are grateful to them." What commendation! This couple saw past their egos and hidden agendas and resolved to work as a team. They had a goal and a purpose for their lives. The best part about working together or being a team is that we appreciate one another more, spend time together and above all grow deeper in intimacy. How many of us start off with great plans of how wonderful we would be to our spouses; how beautiful and peaceful we would make our homes and so on and get distracted by one fad about life or the other? We suddenly want to be like our neighbours: Our homes must be like theirs; we must own similar property or even have better than theirs! We must behave the same way and our spouses must treat us in the same way theirs treat them. The surprising thing is that we forget the grass is always greener on the other side until we actually walk on it! Since we are just looking in, we have no idea what their lives are like and we should understand too that we are different and have dreams of our own. We do not have to be like them!

I am not implying here that for us to succeed in marriage, we must all become tentmakers! This is not so! We can engage in our profession or calling and still serve God effectively! This example was to help us see how important unity between husband and wife is. They channelled their energies to being the best they could be for the Lord and themselves. They were in the true sense "heirs together of the grace of life," as stated in (1 Peter 3:7).

Nothing has changed on God's side. His intention for marriage is still the same: He still wants marriages to be successful, and above all, for Him to be glorified in our homes and our lives. He wants us to fulfill the roles he had crafted for us as their fulfillment is very rewarding, especially when done with great understanding, love, care, and a reverence for God. Anything short of this would only lead to discontentment and a lack of happiness and fulfillment. This is reinforced in the passage from the Bible where the Lord God said, "It is not good for man to be alone; I will make a helper suitable for Him" (Genesis 2:18-The New International Version (NIV) Because God, in His infinite wisdom, used the word *helper,* signifying exactly what relationship He intended this to be—a relationship between two people with a common goal who have decided to spend their lifetime together, living very rich and fulfilling lives, loving and caring for each other, till death do them part. It was not meant for the home to become a war zone!

Genesis 2:24 states that "a man shall leave his father and his mother and cleave to his wife, and they shall become one flesh." As a teenage girl with a very inquisitive and vivid imagination, this sounded strange and farfetched. I often wondered what being one flesh really meant. Did one have to diminish in some way and then become the other person? How would that really be possible since they were still two separate individuals? I spent time looking closely at my parents, careful they never noticed the confusion going on in my mind! I realized they shared some physical attributes as well as some mannerisms and, in some ways, behaved almost identically especially when they were together! I could not help but try paying attention to other couples around me to highlight their similarities. Can you imagine the dismay I felt if I could not find some similarities between them? So, this in no way helped in clearing my confusion. I marvelled at this and my imagination ran riot! How did my parents achieve this feat? What did it really mean, then, that a man and woman became "one flesh" in marriage?

As with most childish mysteries, the answers always come to us when we reach the proper age of maturity! Things became clearer as I became an adult! I knew then that the most obvious way was through sex. This is borne out in 1 Corinthians 6:16 when

Paul says even a man with a prostitute becomes one flesh with her. The mere act of sex is a manifestation of "one flesh" physically and an emblem for the other ways a married couple becomes joined together.

We all know that the physical part of life involves generally maintaining what we have (tending, as stated in the Bible): feeding, housing, repairing and so on. So, another way a man and woman become one flesh in marriage is when they share or take part in performing or caring out these responsibilities as a team. The man is called to leave his parents, which is a physical portrayal of stepping out of their home and taking up the responsibility of providing for his wife. As a result, they embark on the lifelong journey of becoming one flesh with one another. As they begin to work together in the fulfillment of life's responsibilities, they become united, and may even start to look like each other.

The most vital way for being "one flesh" is when a married couple coordinates their efforts to ensure they get the work done for the good of their home, both as individuals and as a team. In the process of raising kids, being active members of the church, working, and seeing friends, husbands and wives can only fulfill their God-given duties if they determine to work together.

It is also necessary that we realize that our body belongs to our spouse. As we can see here in 1 Corinthians 7:4, "the wife does not have authority over her own body but yields it to her husband. In the same way, the husband does not have authority over his own body but yields it to his wife."

So, the way we treat our body reflects the respect we have for our spouse. In our present world, this might sound outdated and even crazy to most of us! However, particular care must be taken with regards to fitness, hairstyles, alcohol consumption or drugs, tattoos, beards, breast implants and the likes. To put it plainly, our spouse must be considered before such decisions are made, as falling into poor health through negligence directly affects the lifestyle of our spouse too. Asking for input regarding clothes is in no way trying to stifle or strip us of our freedom as the world would try to make us believe; this only shows that we care how our spouse sees us. This also applies to physical behaviour. Bear in mind that it is disrespectful to flirt, dress revealingly, or in any other way use our body and actions to portray in any way that we are not one flesh with our spouse.

We live in a world that teaches that our body is our own, to use and treat as we deem fit. The world insists we have to look a certain way or do certain things with our body in order to fit in. It does not endorse the concept of a united home and will try to also lure us away from living the Christian life in the name of freedom, independence, and our democratic rights or what is inherently ours. God stated that, in marriage, husband and wife become one flesh, to live together, cherish and honour each other with their bodies, while serving Him with their combined lives.

The Bible in no way says marriage is mandatory. God does not plan for everyone to marry as we see in 1 Corinthians 7:38: "So then, he who marries the virgin does right, but he who does not marry her does better." We can see a lot of people in the Bible who did not marry but still lived fulfilled lives, serving the Lord fervently. It is very sad to see that marriage has become a new trend or fad with people just wanting to be married without pausing to contemplate what being married entails!

This might sound like an overused phrase, but have we ever paused and contemplated the intent behind these words *helper* or *helpmeet,* as some translations have it? Due to human beings' selfishness, pride, and entitlement, things like men being superior to women and feminism cropped into life. When looked at closely, there was no intent here for one to lord it over the other. God never intended there to be a time when women would need to fight for their rights or freedom! This union was between two souls committed to the common goal of just being present for one another, praying and lifting each other up when the need arose. The Bible further enjoins that "husbands in the same way be considerate as you live with your wives and treat them with respect as the weaker partner and as heirs with you of the gracious gift of life so that nothing will hinder your prayers" (1 Peter 3:7). I am forced to asked, in this day and age, how many husbands can truly boast of being respectful of their wives unless they contribute substantially and economically to the home? The verse here meant being present for, bringing out the best in each other and making a beautiful home comprised of children born out of love and a deep passion and desire for each other. The result then would be that as they honour God and work according to His command, the God who is love would fill them with such love for each other and make them suddenly realize that they are so incomplete without each other but very powerful when they are together—a glorious and beautiful relationship at work!

Genesis 1:26 goes further: "Let us make man in our own image, in our likeness and let them rule over the fish of the sea and the birds of the air." God created humans in His image to rule over other animals, and the Bible goes on to say that "for this reason shall a man leave his father and mother and be united with his wife and the two shall become one flesh." Most of us miss this divine equation because we fail to understand what God desires for marriage. How can we really become one flesh until we resolve to feel each other's pain, work in each other's shoes and be really present for one another? Some of our concepts prior to marriage just centre on the wedding ceremony. It must be the best wedding ever witnessed—with all the trappings from the designer dresses, the food, décor and above all the fanfare that goes with this! The concept of this alone occupies our minds, and we are on cloud nine while planning our whole lives around one day. I am not trying to say planning a great wedding is in any way wrong, but we spare no thought for what happens after the wedding day! Simple things like living together, being present for each other, finances etc. do not feature until after the wedding. When it is all done, we suddenly wake up to the stark reality that we are meant to live or cohabit together as man and wife! We are at a loss as to what is expected of us now. It is like somebody poured a glass of ice over our heads because we were never prepared for this. We start thinking of what should have been thought about before saying "I do." This is where the trouble begins as the scales start falling off our eyes and we realize that this is more than we bargained for. We had jumped in before looking.

I had a friend who said she went on a trip and met a very handsome guy. They partied all night and the next thing she knew they were getting married! The euphoria lasted until they moved in together and she realized she was not prepared for all that! A year later, she was still awaiting the separation to be complete. This is just an example of how casually marriage is being treated! We see it as something we can get in and get out of at will; that there are no limitations nor barriers to what we can or cannot do; that we are not accountable to anyone as it is our lives! We are really mistaken if this is our thought process. God is at the head of marriage and we are answerable to Him, even those who do not believe in Him, for we were created by Him and He has plans for us! If we do not find our bearings quickly, disillusionment sets in and, as couples, we miss God's best that He has destined for us because we do not know what His desires are for our marriages. How do we work on something when we do not even know what we want from it or its value? It is as simple as giving a treasure to a scoundrel or hooligan to take care of. It is destined to be misused and abused. The result of marrying outside the will of God, therefore, would be divorce or an unfulfilled and sad marriage.

As stated previously, marriage is a divine ordinance, which makes it a prime target for attacks from the devil because the devil would rather destroy this institution than see it thrive and bring glory to God. As a result, the devil is constantly at war with couples, tearing down anything that seems to be binding and strengthening this union. So, it is amazing and troubling at the same time that instead of facing the real enemy of our lives, the one who is determined to see us lose, we decide to face the one person that is on our team: our wife or husband!

"For I hate divorce," says the LORD, the God of Israel, "and him who covers his garment with wrong," says the LORD of hosts. "So take heed to your spirit, that you do not deal treacherously."

—Malachi 2:16

Chapter Two

The Creator's Design

What really was God's intention for instituting the concept of marriage in creation? How did He want or intend for us to carry this on? What was its purpose? What were the guidelines? A look at the Bible tells us.

God made one woman from Adam's rib even though He still had ribs for two or more—His ideal union was just between one man and one woman, nothing else! He wanted this unity so that couples would find fulfillment in themselves and each other, children could be brought up in the right way, love and trust would thrive in the home, couples and families would live in one accord and worship God in their daily work and lives. What then went wrong? Why do marriages fail? Why has divorce become a better option and why have human beings changed the concept, definition, and purpose of marriage? Why have we suddenly turned this union into a mockery?

If you are not sure of your decision to marry and stay so for life, then it is better not to go into it.

God's intention for marriage was good as is clearly stated in Jeremiah 29:11, thus; "For I know the plans I have for you," declares the LORD, "plans to prosper you and not to harm you, plans to give you hope and a future." We see here that God's purpose and plan for marriage were good. He had conceived of creation and marriage was an aspect of this. He wanted man to live a fulfilled life, and he also wanted to prosper couples through this union and not hurt them. So, in order to have this happen, marriage was to be a lifelong commitment. Marriage was meant to be for as long as both of you were alive! Remember the phrase "till death do us part"? God intended that man and woman commit to a permanent relationship in marriage, creating a bond that was to last a lifetime. Divorce was not a consideration here as stated explicitly in Malachi 2:16: "For I hate divorce," says the LORD, the God of Israel, "and him who covers his garment with wrong," says the LORD of hosts. "So, take heed to your spirit, that you do not deal treacherously."

It could not be any clearer. We are being told here that God hates divorce. It was only instituted by Moses to protect the injured party and only in cases of adultery within marriage; it was not to be used as a cop-out. For a divorce to be possible, approval by a judge was required after it was proven beyond every measurable doubt that a partner had been unfaithful.

This brings us to a very profound contemplation: Why was this the only reason given for divorce? Could it not be done in a way that we just walk out when we are tired of each other? Well, the reason here is very simple: God hates the sin of adultery and fornication because they defile marriages. Adultery practically means another person has been brought into the marriage that was meant to be between two people only. This could be through extramarital sex or other amorous relationships, which is a violation of the very concept of marriage. Contrary to popular opinion, a sexual relationship outside marriage is frowned upon and condemned. It is shown to be very destructive and not only defiles the marital bed but is absolutely condemned by God. He wants us to honour and worship Him in our marriages and Hebrews 13:4 says: "Marriage should be honored by all, and the marriage bed kept pure, for God will judge the adulterer and all the sexually immoral."

Leviticus 18:20 enjoins us, "Do not have sexual relations with your neighbor's wife and defile yourself with her." Due to the pervasion that has cropped up in marriages, either spouse can do such things and come home, bringing defilement to the marriage and the marriage bed. Such a person defiles Christian marriage, even if the corruption is only in thought. Most people, especially men, see nothing wrong with this. They expect their wives to be faithful in marriage, but they themselves engage in adultery, prostitution, and other types of sexual immorality. It must not be forgotten here that anything that comes between the physical bond of marriage has the ability to break it. This could be in the form of infidelity or death.

Jesus said in Matthew 19:8 that "Moses permitted you to divorce your wives because your hearts were hard. But it was not this way from the beginning. I tell you that anyone who divorces his wife, except for sexual immorality, and marries another woman commits adultery."

We see in the Old Testament that God allowed divorce if a man's heart became so hardened against his wife that she was actually better off without him; however, this was not a very common occurrence then and as Jesus mentioned, this was not God's intent for marriage. Marriage was to be a permanent illustration of God's love and devotion to Israel. Can it be a reflection of God's love if a man is cruel or abusive to his wife? Is he reflecting the kind, forgiving spirit of God? We must bear in mind that if a man divorces his wife under such circumstances he is not to marry again; the Bible depicts God's faithfulness despite Israel's incessant spiritual adultery as stated in Malachi 2:14: "You ask, 'Why?' It is because the LORD is the witness between you and the wife of your youth. You have been unfaithful to her, though she is your partner, the wife of your marriage covenant." It is further reinforced in Malachi 2:16 that "the man who hates and divorces his wife...does violence to the one he should protect." Put simply, this meant that a man who couldn't love his wife as God loved Israel was not worthy of getting a new wife.

So, what can we get from this? It is undoubtedly reflected here that a man, no matter what he felt like, was not to divorce his wife unless she was unfaithful, or he was abusive, and the divorce was protection for the wife. If the divorce was not because of unfaithfulness on her part, he was not allowed to remarry, as seen in Matthew 19:9: "I tell you that anyone who divorces his wife, except for sexual immorality, and marries another woman commits adultery." So, how can we in all sincerity justify divorce by saying we have *"fallen out of love, or she/he is no longer my type and so on?"* What happened to the privilege of being believing spouses who are assumed to be led by the Holy Spirit, not by their own selfish desires. Are we as believers not supposed to be led by the Spirit of God that works through us, sanctifying us and enabling us to grow from glory to glory in our bid to be more like Christ?

Why do we suddenly forget that marriage was ordained by God and He wants us to resolve any issue that would otherwise lead to divorce? It is an added advantage if both spouses are humble, patient, kind and loving, and have a healthy Spirit and supportive church to provide and equip them with adequate tools to successfully live loving and caring lives and as a result, help them navigate through any issue the devil might seek to use in destroying them. God wanted couples to be married so they could provide each other with companionship. The Bible encourages self-control as we can see in the following passage in 1 Corinthians 7:5; Do not deprive one another, except perhaps by agreement for a limited time, that you may devote yourselves to prayer; but then come together again, so that satan may not tempt you because of your lack of self-control, marriage should never be only built on sexual passion as this can never stand the test of time nor would it be strong in any way. When one partner cheats on the other, it is very traumatic for the cheated. You start questioning everything about you. Most times you start wondering if it was because of you or something you did or failed to do that drove him/her to the other person. You can taste betrayal on your tongue and feel it rumbling, tearing away in the pit of your stomach. You feel so used and violated to the extent that you might lose faith in yourself and everybody around you. The first question you ask yourself is *Why?* and this is within reason. After all, you were very invested in this marriage. You did everything right. Betrayal was the last thing you thought about; you had the perfect marriage or so you thought, and your spouse made promises to you! It hits you where you never thought possible, sometimes leaving you so bitter and distraught, wondering what you can do next! You cannot even comprehend nor explain how you feel to another person as it strips you of all, to the extent that you are on the brink of losing even your self-esteem and sanity.

Well, if this happens you must learn to forgive, no matter how much pain you have been dealt nor how hurtful it is. Take it to the Lord and ask him to teach you how to forgive and He will. Forgiving is the best option because if you do not, you will be stuck where you are, wallowing in self-pity and unforgiveness, and it will inadvertently hinder your life and marriage. Forgiving and leaving everything to the Lord will give you peace of mind. He will bring about restoration and healing in your lives and make you able to carry on.

Let us assume we have two pieces of paper glued together—one of these will be a man and the other a woman. After gluing them together, we then let them dry up and later try separating these pieces of paper from each other as carefully as possible. We can try all possible tricks, but the result would be that no matter how careful we are in this process, either piece can never be returned to its former state; in short, it is near impossible to get them back to how they were before. There would always be parts ripped off from each paper left on the other. There can never be a clean break. The same can be said for divorce.

You must be wondering what this has in common with marriage. I will try as much as possible to make this analogy easier to understand. You see, on the journey toward intimacy with one another and as the couples are united and become one, there is bound to be some spiritual exchange taking place; some deposits from the man or woman are transferred to the other partner. This is to enable the equation of the two becoming one possible; they are no longer two separate entities, but two bodies sharing one soul. As stated in the Bible, "The two shall become one." Just like we tried making the papers one and later separating them, divorce leaves a lot of brokenness, hurt, regret, scarring, and a lot more is left behind, especially if there are children involved.

The two, remember, had become intimate on the journey of becoming one flesh as the Lord had enjoined! So, a few of each partner's attributes are left in the other. How then is it possible to remove them so they can be separate? It is a separation that can never be complete nor put behind us as we are always being advised to do by the judges and marriage counsellors. In Mark 10:9, the Bible reminds us here that when two become one, let no one separate them. It is also daunting to note that society today glorifies adultery, fornication, lesbianism, homosexuality, bisexuality, pedophilia, and other forms of sexual deviations. Every type of sexual perversion is applauded and made to look like the order of the day. Some of the more shocking ones are those who believe that it is their right to swap their partners whenever they feel the need. We must not forget that the Bible tells us that God wants us to honour monogamous, lifelong marriages. He opposes all who oppose and despise marriage through pervasion, adultery and fornication.

It is not only destructive but also sinful to enter into a marriage with the idea that if it is not going to work, or if it is not as we hoped for, we can easily end it. I have often heard people say, "I just want my life back, I need a break!" Where was your life before this? Why was this not taken into consideration before you decided to tie the knot? The truth, no matter how hurtful it is, is that we have suddenly become too entitled and self-absorbed! It must be about *me:* my ideas, feelings, wants, and what works best for me, man or woman! This is all wrong! Our intention, once we start contemplating marriage and when we finally do get married, should be that it is going to be for life and no matter the storms that may prevail against our marriages, we must resolve to make our marriages work. We must stand by one another and weather these storms together because marriages were meant to last till death do us part! Be empathetic and learn to work in each other's shoes. What relationship does not require a great deal of investment from both individuals engaged in it to succeed? Right from when we announce the union, words like *hitch* and the like should be disposed of. You might want to ask why. This is because when we hitch something to another, it implies that it is not going to remain there forever! Take for example a trailer hitched to a truck. Would you leave it like that forever? No! This is because there would come a time when you would need to unhitch it and stow it away until you needed it again, especially during the winter and when the storms of life raged. Can you stow away your spouse until you need her again? So why use such a word to denote marriage?

Commitment and permanence should be our goal in marriage. There will be storms because two separate individuals with different orientations and backgrounds have been brought together in marriage. How possible is it for two different people to co-exist without having a little conflict, misunderstanding, or disagreement? Even the best of friends disagree on certain issues! We must, however, understand that these disagreements are not meant to break our relationships but to make them stronger.

We reveal our true self when faced with conflict. Some of us have particularly mastered the art of fighting dirty. As we all know, sparks are bound to fly, especially when two entirely different people are in a long-lasting relationship together. We know how to strip each other of all dignity and really hit below the belt! May I state here that in times of conflict, only the right mindset will help us weather the storms and challenges? We are endowed with a very wonderful attribute from God, which is our gift of choice. When at a crossroads, we can either decide to fight fairly and cleanly and stay or be as dirty as we possibly can get, give up the fight to preserve our marriage before it even begins, then leave, as not being able to imagine being in that relationship a minute longer!

A relationship that is based on respect for one another, love, trust, and above all, the fear and love of God, will always stand the test of time. In friendship, do we just call it quits because we had a disagreement or a misunderstanding and never come back again? Why do we put greater effort into working things out with our friends but throw in the towel at the first sign of disagreement when it comes to marriage with our best friend—our spouse? The Bible enjoins us in Ephesians 4:26 (English Standard Version) to "be angry and do not sin; do not let the sun go down on your anger." When you hear spouses discuss each other, you might be forced into thinking they are talking about some archenemy or some villain! I once witnessed two friends talking about their respective spouses and could not hide my dismay and shock! I will refrain from repeating their words here! How do you expect your friends or loved ones to have any respect for your spouses if you go around bad-mouthing and belittling them! Proverbs12:4 says, "An excellent wife is the crown of her husband, but she who brings shame is like rottenness in his bones." After discrediting each other to this extent, you expect to have a flourishing relationship? This is impossible! You will find out that the joy you have been looking for just keeps slipping by and you will not know when you have actually chased it away through your actions. You must be ready to give your best in a marriage. When you love your spouse, you pay attention to them and work to build the relationship. You nurture it until it starts blooming, you value your spouse and would not want to give up anything you are invested in. So, deciding to abandon ship and leave the marriage is not an option because you are in for the long haul.

Bear in mind:

> Love is patient, love is kind. It does not envy, it does not boast, it is not proud. It does not dishonor others, it is not self-seeking, it is not easily angered, it keeps no record of wrongs. Love does not delight in evil but rejoices with the truth. It always protects, always trusts, always hopes, always perseveres. (1 Corinthians 13:4–8).

And to add to this: Love does not violate the one he loves!

If love is all that is exemplified above, why then have we suddenly cheapened it by becoming selfish, entitled and manipulative all in the name of love? The Almighty God, in His infinite wisdom, knew the mindset and temperament of His children and put everything in place to guide us through this huge responsibility of relationships and choice. Just as we try not to play mind games with our friends, we must also not do the same thing with our spouses. Forgive me here if I sound so happy-go-lucky! I know that sometimes circumstances in marriage can test you to almost your limits where you start wondering if your spouse is just plain stupid! Why can't he or she see what is so clearly visible? Are you the only one endowed with the intelligence to understand right from wrong? You are forced sometimes where his/her intelligence and reasoning prowess have all disappeared. Trust me when I say that you are not perfect either. This is so true just by the mere fact that you are married to your spouse! I bet you, he sometimes feels you are not making sense too! We must understand that whatever we are is by the grace of God. Instead of beating ourselves up over who is wrong or right, ask Him for wisdom and He will surely provide and guide you in your choices.

We would be setting ourselves up for failure if we thought fighting and nagging would make our spouses change. If anything, these actions will only drive a wedge between a couple. Even though change is a natural aspect of life, we cannot change someone; the only change that is sustainable and enduring must start from us. Then and only then will we get desirable results.

Trust in the Lord with all your heart and lean not on your own understanding; in all your ways submit to him, and he will make your paths straight.

—Proverbs 3:6

Chapter Three

Me + You = Us
Rewriting Your
Preconceived Notions
of Marriage

Saying I do is the easiest part of marriage, and you can choose to say it in any language or way you love! In fact, the more dramatic you make it, the more you will impress your audience. Is that a guarantee for a successful marriage? Are you getting married to please an audience? Why then should you go to such lengths to please people who could not be bothered if you lived or died?

Prior to marriage and taking the vows, it is all about you! Your happiness, dreams, ambitions, goals, and so on! Well, when you fall in love, it is like a bolt of lightning hits you. Suddenly, your thinking begins to shift. You begin to think about another person aside from yourself and all the fantasies you had tucked away come to the fore. This is no wonder because you have lived your life all this while thinking about what makes you happy and fulfilled. It has always been about you and now you must incorporate him or her (your beloved) into your thought process.

When you were born, your life was just reflected as an empty canvas. This canvas was open for the caregivers or others you, as a child, interacted with to draw or write on. Whatever experience you were exposed to, good or bad, left a mark on the canvas because, as a child, you soaked up everything and stowed this unconsciously away on the canvas, which played a vital part in shaping and forming your life. As you grew and started interacting and making choices for yourself, you began to write a script based on your expectations, choices, and experiences. If you experienced abuse, rejection, brokenness, or molestation of any kind, you would bring the pattern or legacy of this into your marriage. This is because you would not only have constructed them as protective shields, but they would have become a very vital part of your life: some serving as mechanisms for self-preservation while others as mere fantasies that could be put away. After all, you have to look out for yourself, so you do not ever have to be vulnerable again. You become so entangled in these self-preservative webs you are building around you. You act them out so well that they become a vital part of you and when you get married, you are incapable of letting go and giving your best to your marriage and life. You become negatively impacted.

As you introduce or bring them into your life, they become patterns that show up in all aspects of your being. They are accepted by you and others as a part of who you are; you do not acknowledge these things as being destructive in your life because this is all you have ever been aware of. You do not see the effect they have on your life. Little wonder then that both the husband and the wife, even when similarly raised, have different scripts, which may or may not contain the perfect idea for marriage. This is because of our individual differences. God has made each one of us unique and special in our own way. No two people can ever be entirely the same. So, the scripts would have dreams, goals, perceived characteristics of the perfect husband or wife or the perfect home, children, and so on. The world has made it even worse now that we have the option of choosing our children's IQs, gender, and even their physical attributes. We might even decide to clone them in the future!

I heard a friend say that the guy she marries would have to wait upon her hand and foot and above all serve her breakfast in bed. She must be cuddled all day and made to feel loved! This was her condition for a successful marriage! Well, there is no harm in dreaming or having such notions, but what happens to the other partner's dreams, goals, ambitions, and finances? Do not forget that you are two different entities with different personalities and interests. Would he have this as part of his script too? Where would they get the income to live on and build a home if all they do is cuddle up to each other?

Understanding this comes highly priced now and sometimes very late in a relationship. There is a lopsided concept to this. One spouse should understand that the other is incapable of making the other fulfilled. The power lies within each one of us and cannot be achieved through another person. Going into any relationship with the idea that another person is the reason for our happiness and is going to make us feel better is wrong and the greatest ill we can do to ourselves.

Our Mixed-up Idea of Married Love

We are in love with the idea of love, especially the romantic love depicted in movies and novels, which portrays marriage as a breeze. More often than not, this depiction falls short and clashes with the love that is enduring and is supposed to stand the test of time in our marriages. With this script, we expect our partners to be all-sufficient for us and reminiscent of all romantic idols in these movies. They must meet all our needs, be at our beck and call. We also have the wrong thinking that our spouses are supposed to be our supermen or superwomen and must meet all our demands, expectations, and goals. On top of this, we think they have been vested with the responsibility of making us happy! When this does not happen, we become disillusioned and disappointed and the blame game now starts.

The mere thought that another person is or should be responsible for our happiness, as I mentioned earlier, is very wrong. Our spouse is human and that means that he or she is not perfect! In as much as we cannot see this beyond our rose-tinted glasses, our spouse is as human as they come! This means that just as humans have failures, he does too! He will fall sick, fail to meet your expectations, and let you down sometimes by forgetting things you never thought anybody who professes to love you should. Much to your surprise, you thought you knew every tiny bit about him and suddenly you realize your idea of fun is very different from his. If anything, you are very different from each other both in temperament and lifestyle! How else would you explain the behaviour of someone who thinks something like a game night for both of you is lame!

Many conflicts in homes or marriages stem from false notions, scripting, or assumptions concerning the way we perceive that things should be around our homes. We forget that no man on Earth has been created with the superpower to meet all our needs.

So, what do you do? You have suddenly realized that all your preconceived notions on the script are just a figment of your imagination. For all purposes, you have been living in an unreal world that revolved all around the romantic dreams you have been weaving! First, you must recognize that you are each different and begin working toward a common goal. This difference is not geared toward destroying you but turning both of you into a formidable team. Half of the battle is won as soon as you realize that you are in it together. Men have not been vested with the power to control your happiness or provide it for you. Happiness is a choice! No one can make this choice for you! You can decide to be happy or wallow in self-pity. However, there is one thing you can do for yourself: turn to the Almighty God, our Creator, the one who "knows all about us and knows what we need before we even ask" (Matthew 6:8) to meet your needs for validation, self-esteem, and so on! He alone can provide all we need, even the super being we are searching for!

I know a friend who already has her life mapped out: from the birth of her children to their names and the years leading up to these events. She has figured out all she thinks would make her life fulfilled: all that she thinks her ideal family, children, husband, and home would be like. I am not saying it is entirely wrong to have an idea in mind of what you want; the wrong thing here is that you are forgetting that your spouse also has a mind of his own and dreams as you do! It is not necessary that all that is written on this script is right. There is no problem with marriage; it's our intention and the people involved in a marriage that cause the problem. How else can you explain the fact that after being married for thirty-something years, you have still not been able to unite and really begin to work toward intimacy with your spouse? You suddenly realize you want to get out of the marriage! What happened? Why did you have a change of heart? My take here is that we need God's grace to see us through all challenges. Nothing good ever comes easy without the Lord and hard work.

Our perception of marriage has changed, and this has a lot to do with whether we have successful marriages or not. Your mind-set on getting married and staying true to the vows has a big role to play in marital success. A teenage girl once told me that she saw no valid reason to marry when she could have much more without the constraints of this institution. This made me begin to wonder what she perceived marriage to be. Did she see it as an institution that the Lord God meant it to be, or like a prison that would stifle her progress?

What made her think this way? Could it be she had been jaded by all the failed marriages around her? She was already skeptical about marriage before even being ready for it. We could say here that there are many options available to her if she fails at marriage. Should she even attempt to get married with this mindset? What would she become after this trial and error?

Do not forget that the divorce mentality as an escape route, which is readily available, is part of this script because who wants to be saddled with a spouse who does not fit into the ideal that has been scripted?

When you get married and you vow "Till death do us part," you say the words, and you see in them an ideal to aspire to, something we all long to attain, and yet not all of us do. You have not thought it all out! You know the worst part? These scripts are not discarded but taken along into marriage.

I would ask a pertinent question here: What is marriage? According to our previous definition, it is the union between a man and a woman, as ordained by God.

When people get married and become "husbands and wives," they forget to rewrite these scripts as a couple, highlighting their dreams, aspiration and goals for their marriage. Each person sticks to his or her script and then tries to implement whatever was written on it in the marriage without considering the other partner. Because these scripts were written when you were both single, there immediately is a break or breach in the marriage. You find out that when you individually try to implement what was on the script, it falls short of your expectations. The fairy tale is disrupted, and marriage becomes very unappealing. You start imposing your will on your spouse, and if this fails, you resort to blackmail and mind games. Consequently, dissatisfaction sets into the marriage and one thing leads to another. You suddenly realize that this was not in your write-up; the scripts are not working as they should for you! This is contrary to the expectation of marriage, and what you find yourself in falls short. The relationship is no longer appealing to you. The reasonable thought process would be to work on it, try changing the script to suit both of you, but marriage according to these individual scripts did not make any mention of this.

Nowhere was it written that marriage was supposed to require hard work! Maybe you are just not very lucky after all; everyone must have expectations that are working for them. That explains why they are all so happy and you are not! This was not a prerequisite at all!

Hmmm … It is now time to wake up to the understanding that this is the real world, not some fairytale land, where it was just about you! Okay, the pronoun has changed—it is about *us* (*we*); *I* and *me* have lost their place of pride! You are dealing with real beings, not robots! For success, both of you need to sit down and have a heart-to-heart chat and then resolve to rewrite your scripts for the success of your marriage. You are going to write just one script, not two individual ones, because now you are on a mission to win and together you will have to succeed! You resolve that you must make this marriage work. Do not hold onto the individual scripts. You are going to start a new canvas or painting, and this is going to be just about the two of you—your plans, goals, aspirations and dreams for your lives—and, of course, with God at the helm. Remember that a painting that is started but not worked on every day till it is done can never become a masterpiece! So now you need to work hard, with utmost sincerity, trust, and love to make this a great one. As I mentioned earlier, while the work can be hard, it shouldn't make you miserable. It should be enjoyable work and it should feel rewarding and not make you stressed beyond belief. It should be like building your very own dream house! You are excited and you keep coming up with new ideas because this is going to be your haven. You feel exhilarated. You want to make sure it is done perfectly! Exactly how you want it! On this beautiful journey, be careful to make the best of it for both of you. It is a combined effort that will make it long-lasting and truly beautiful. So out with the king/queen mentality and in with the protector and helper.

Marriage does not work in a day. It is a journey of a lifetime for both of you. If one partner falls, both of you will fall too. This journey cannot be undertaken alone. You need each other's support. Invest your time with each other, seek the Lord for direction, forgive immediately, and be one another's strength and support. As you progress on this canvas or script, you start including family (in-laws). Yes, you are not married only to your spouse; they come with a package! They have a past! Your spouse was raised and brought up by someone and you do not expect your spouse to just abandon them because you are married. Your spouse is somebody's son/daughter, brother/sister, and has responsibilities toward them. So, this is a good time to decide what you are going to do. Are you going to have them in your lives or abandon them as is the case these days? Then, if you want, you can have children. I have met a lot of couples who have opted out of having children for one reason or another. I am happy with that because I think it is better not to have them than to do so when you know you are not fit mentally, physically, or emotionally, and cannot or due to some constraints might not be able to take care of them.

You go into marriage expecting the same kind of love you give in return and you ultimately feel cheated because you are focused on the ideal relationship you want. Do not set yourself up for failure! It is most likely not going to happen according to your expectations. A wise man once told me that I should marry someone who loves me more than I love him because, he said, "It is a great blessing if you are loved twice as much as you love your spouse." It left me wondering what would become of the spouse then? Does he or she have feelings?

Another misconception is going into marriage thinking that your spouse's love is going to make up for your lack of love for yourself. This is not right because you should love yourself more. How else are you going to love someone else if you fail to love you? How can you give what you do not have? Learn to love yourself first, and the right person God has created for you will come along and love you as you deserve to be loved. It may take a lot of work, patience, and prayers, but what God has meant for you will seek you out! Trust God; He has greater plans for you. Seek His will in all you do, and He will show you which path to take.

Marriage is a God-ordained ministry and we should not enter into it if we know we are not capable of fulfilling it as designed by God.

Two are better than one,
    because they have a good return
    for their labor:
If either of them falls down,
    one can help the other up.
But pity anyone who falls
    and has no one to help them up.
Also, if two lie down together, they
will keep warm.
    But how can one keep warm alone?
Though one may be overpowered,
    two can defend themselves.
A cord of three strands is not quickly
broken.

—Ecclesiastes 4:9–12

Chapter Four

Where the Help Meets

Is there a need for there to be unity and understanding in the home? Is there a need to perform certain roles in the home? How many of you really get married and are ready to do the work needed to make it a success? Does it really matter if we do nothing? My answer here will be a resounding, Yes!

You must agree these are a lot of questions, but they all have their answers in the Bible. A careful look at Genesis 1 reveals that in marriage, you are equal partners of God's gifts and benefits. A wise man once told me that marriages were made in heaven and each spouse was preordained, carefully chosen, and crafted just for the other by God. If this is the case, then why do we have so many divorces, or why are couples just ready to throw in the towel at a moment's notice? Is divorce the best option? Did God intend this from the beginning? I bet you that was not God's intention. Our God is not a god of failure or incomplete projects.

The Bible says in Philippians 1:6, "Being confident of this, that he who began a good work in you will carry it on to completion until the day of Jesus Christ." He has destined all of us for greatness and He knows what we need to get us where He wants us. The question then is whether we want to go along with Him or chart our own paths. These things, as mentioned earlier, happen because we fail to seek God's face and wait upon Him for His choice in our lives. We mistake the emotions of attraction and lust for love, and we have no plans and reasons for wanting to get into this marriage and stay there.

You are married but have intentionally left an exit door open, or you have some options tucked neatly away at the back of your mind in case—just in case—it does not work! Who in their right mind starts a good thing with failure in mind? Marriage brings about the union between a husband and a wife who leave all other relationships and become one flesh: "That is why a man leaves his father and mother and is united to his wife, and they become one flesh" (Genesis 2:24 and Ephesians 5:31). They are on a path to making their lives fulfilling and happy as they become each other's strength. On this journey, however, some men get married as they want wives but do not want to be husbands. They want to remain little mommy's boys who are handed everything they need on a platter. In short, if it were possible for them to have their wives wait on them hand and foot, life would be great. So, they get married and are never present as husbands or fathers as they have not transitioned fully from boys to becoming men. They walk in total oblivion of what is expected of them as married men. Why can they not still be dependent on their mothers to wait upon them hand and foot? Why can't their spouses just evolve and become their mothers? Better still, why can they not be left alone to sow their wild oats?

The purpose of marriage is not to increase a man's power, property, or influence or even his dominance over his wife; rather it is intended to glorify and give God pleasure. We give God pleasure when we live intentionally for Him and prosper in our marriages and other areas of His calling. The Bible gives some very specific instructions regarding what individuals must do so their marriages can fulfill God's purpose. Each member must deny their natural self-centred inclinations in favour of what is best for the relationship. Husbands must love with self-sacrifice as stated in Ephesians 5:25 thus; "Husbands, love your wives, just as Christ loved the church and gave himself up for her." It would be apt to say here that as wives, you must bear in mind that you are a member of a team and as with every team, there must be a leader or a head and God has endowed your husband with this special role as clearly seen Ephesians 5:22–23: "Wives, submit yourselves to your own husbands as you do to the Lord. For the husband is the head of the wife as Christ is the head of the church, his body, of which he is the Savior." Wives should also understand that the term "helper" as we see in Genesis 2:18 is not in any way trying to depict them as slaves, maids or administrative assistants. It would be worthwhile for wives to note that you have been bestowed with a huge responsibility. God has called you to be the pillar for the home, endowed with the attributes of a fierce warrior and specially called to protect and defend. You are a bona fide superhero if you answer this call and depend on the Lord to help you through. In fulfilling your role as husband or wife, it is pertinent to note that a marriage can't be successful unless both the wife and husband work together to love and protect each other.

Couples must place a higher value on each other than they do on other relationships or may have done in the past as they work toward a wholesome relationship characterized by love, respect, and the fear of God. Acceptance, avoiding selfishness, and being constantly present are some ingredients needed in this relationship. Learning to be positive is important as negative issues violate marriage and intimacy. So, if you are inclined toward this type of behaviour, this must be discarded. You need to work hard to earn each other's trust, and it would not take time for you to find fulfillment if this is done. You must understand that love is doable while trust is very fragile.

When you have built a strong relationship with your spouse, you get to a stage where you know instinctively what your spouse's reaction would be before anything. Love, honour, and respect for each other thrive in this environment. Children raised in this atmosphere of love and understanding realize at a very early age that their parents are one, and so there is no acting up nor trying to pit one against the other as this would not work. Helpmeet is not only applicable to just physical or manual help but to other aspects of the couple's life too. You can fulfill this role when you trust God.

Both husband and wife must share the same belief system. You must have shared beliefs and values. When you begin your married life with a foundation of strong beliefs and ideals, you will know you need to work every day as partners to make sure that everything is going smoothly and that your values stay aligned no matter what circumstances or challenges you are going through in your lives. Having the same values ensure that you agree on the main issues around your marriage, like raising the children, major purchases, financial obligations, and so on. This is so that you do not have major disagreements when the time comes. Bear in mind that these are not the only issues that may arise, so they are not carved in stone. You might need to address this more as you progress in your marriage.

There is nothing as comforting and fulfilling for the wife and children as when the husband is really fulfilling the role of the religious head of the home. It unleashes confidence in all, and it makes the family actively participate in things related to God. When the husband decides to let the reins loose and the wife steps in, there is the danger that most of the children will decide not to attend church or be involved in religious activities, especially the sons. It makes the wife feel very insignificant, overwhelmed, and alone as she tries to fill the void her husband has left in their religious lives.

It is often the case that this becomes a great challenge when the husband doesn't seem to "obey the Good News." The husband in mind here might be a nonbeliever or he might simply be an insensitive husband who is not treating his wife in the manner Christ would want him to. The wife's key recurring question will be: "Will I decide to manage my husband, or will I decide to let God manage him?" It does not make matters any better when you adhere to the command to accept your husband's authority. You are at a crossroads. Should you stop going to church or not? Is that what we are enjoined to do here? Let us look at what Peter meant!

Accepting the authority of your husband. Since two people cannot form a democracy, someone in a marriage must have the responsibility for leadership. This is not intended to be a "makes all decisions" kind of leadership but the duty to share the decision-making unless a deadlock occurs, at which time God expects the husband to step up and exercise authority. A man is more likely to give his wife's perspective serious consideration if he walks in the fear of the Lord and knows that the tough choices are really going to be left to him. The man must understand what his role is in the home because, how would it be possible for a woman to accept the authority of one who does not even know what God expects of him?

Peter reminded husbands that they must care for their wives and this must be practiced in four areas: He stipulated that the husband was to honour his wife and provide her with emotional security. There is nothing as daunting or intimidating for a woman as the realization that she cannot expect some form of emotional security from her husband. She becomes lonely, insecure, and cannot be emotionally present for her husband when needed. The husband must respect his wife's feelings, thoughts, and desires. He doesn't need to agree with everything she says, but he must understand that the wife has feelings and her mouth is not just for show or just an appendage that completes her appearance! Husbands, do not feel small or intimidated when your wives make an input! They have been placed in your lives to enrich it and bring sanity to those sometimes-chaotic moments that do not seem to make any sense to you. You must seek her judgment and must also respect and honour her right to speak. Remember she has been placed in your life by divine ordinance, so you must not only seek her input but desire it too. This is because God desires sometimes to use your wife to guide you. As a result, he has endowed her with sensitivity and natural cautions that you may not possess.

When you get married, just like Adam, you are on a sweet journey of discovery. Presented with Eve,

Adam could not help but exclaim, "This is indeed bone of my bone, flesh of my flesh. She shall be called *wo-man!*" Did Adam see something more than we can see? Is it possible that upon seeing Eve, he suddenly realized what he had been missing all along? A vital part of him, someone who shared similar characteristics with him but was very different at the same time. He could not help but immediately embark on a journey of discovery. His intention here was to start from the very beginning, get to know and understand this gift of perfection that God had bestowed upon him. Adam did not try to put her in her place; he embraced her as a part of him! I am sure that as soon as he did this, Eve began to let down her guard and welcome him as a part of her. The journey had started for both.

You do not have a choice. For a successful marriage, both of you must determine to understand each other. I did not say you must learn to ignore each other here but to learn tolerance toward each other. In marriage, there will be many times when you do not understand your spouse and may even become frustrated with them. You do not need to worry or beat yourself up for being so unloving. These feelings are not alien to you; they are completely natural. When you are in constant contact and living in such proximity to another person, this is something that is bound to happen.

I remember a lady seeking advice once expressed her dissatisfaction with her husband's nonchalance by saying to me, "My husband is as dumb as they come and is as hard as nails. Sometimes I feel like clobbering him on the head with my frying pan! He does not seem to understand anything I say!" Well, trust me, she was dead serious. She said she could not remember when last they even had a constructive conversation as they always ended up yelling and that always made it easy for her husband to just leave or clamp up. This, as funny as it may sound, is not supposed to take place in a marriage. How do you get things that need both of your attention done? How do you discipline your children or make plans for the future and your life together? Above all, how do you grow in intimacy as a couple?

Another pertinent point in Peter's discourse is that the husband has the very important duty of making sure he understands his wife and helps her understand him! This is not to be taken lightly because no matter how irritable or unapproachable she might be, husbands, you have married her, so you have been bestowed with the delightful challenge to learn to understand your wife. It starts with you paying subtle attention to the little things about her, especially what triggers her action, inaction, or reaction. She is more than just a pretty face and the unpaid housekeeper! It takes a very conscious effort for you to get to know your wife's moods, aspirations, desires, needs, fears, and hopes. You need to listen with everything you have got. As the counsellors put it, you must become a very active listener.

It feels very wonderful and loving if your wife walks into a room and you take a moment to recognize her presence and connect with her on a very intimate level by touch or an unspoken intimate exchange of a glance. It makes both of you feel revitalized and loved. Permit me to say here that a woman who has her husband's attention when she needs it never feels neglected or unloved. She glows and her innermost beauty comes out. She would be like a fresh spring flower that has just opened its petals to receive the early morning sunshine. She would immediately open and bask in the attention she receives. This is the only way you will be able to pick up the cues and hints she is unable to verbalize. Forget second-guessing or believing that when she says she has a headache, it's her way of trying to put you off touching her.

When you really get to know her, you will realize that she can simply be truthful about her desires. You can achieve this by letting her know that you care for her and by treating her like a human being and not some showpiece. Approach her always in an understanding, caring, and loving way.

When we talk of marriage, what comes immediately to mind? The fact that it is a union! That means both of you would have to live together and be united! You would have to do things that would be beneficial to both of you and bring glory to the Lord. It should be an intentional desire in this relationship, bearing or considering each other's feelings, needs, and wants. It goes beyond this to you becoming empathetic toward one another, feeling what your partner feels. This invariably means that one person would have to give up a known and familiar home and move into an unknown one. This is because marriage is a physical relationship; it transcends just sharing accommodation and sometimes, splitting the rent and is much more than sharing the same address.

Marriage cannot happen in a vacuum, and without a fundamental physical relationship, it is a union of body and mind. Both of you are going to be united, as put aptly in the Bible in Mark 10:8: "and the two are united into one." So, we have to remove our focus from 'I' we, us and ours. This is where we begin the journey to real intimacy and the process of actually becoming 'One' as this does not just happen after the exchange of wedding vows. Since they have declared that they are no longer two but one, it is now time to intentionally put effort into making this union work. The first step is to put our spouse's needs above ours. We then must consciously work towards developing intimacy on several levels, especially physical intimacy where the couple strive to become one by communicating love through simple gestures like an occasional touch, showing appreciation, support when needed and being present for one another. In trying to develop or build emotional intimacy with our spouse, we must learn to willingly expose ourselves emotionally. A note of warning to both husband and wife here; when your spouse exposes her feelings and is vulnerable, this is not a sign for you to make a mockery of them. Make sure to create a safe environment where each person feels safe and secure to open up. Both husband and wife must also work towards Spiritual intimacy as they actively put Christ in the centre of their lives and marriage. They must desist from developing intimacies outside the marriage and, as mentioned before, focus on each other exemplifying Christ in all they do. He has made it possible for us that through the knowledge of Him, we are not only heirs to the throne, but also as Christian couples, enjoy a deeper spiritual relationship, as seen in 1 Corinthians 7:1–5:

> Now for the matters you wrote about: "It is good for a man not to have sexual relations with a woman." But since sexual immorality is occurring, each man should have sexual relations with his own wife, and each woman with her own husband. The husband should fulfill his marital duty to his wife, and likewise the wife to her husband. The wife does not have authority over her own body but yields it to her husband. In the same way, the husband does not have authority over his own body but yields it to his wife. Do not deprive each other except perhaps by mutual consent and for a time, so that you may devote yourselves to prayer. Then come together again so that Satan will

not tempt you because of your lack of self-control.

A truly spiritual husband will fulfill his marital duties and love his wife. God created man and woman and assigned different roles to each. He made it possible for them to partner and partake in God's gifts. He never designed one to be inferior to the other in the central place of life; their access to God in the spiritual, physical, or emotional aspect of the relationship was not restricted to gender. God loved them both the same—both husband and wife have equal standing and are equal partners in God's gift. Therefore, when both are growing closer to God, they inevitably grow closer to each other. Praying together and living spiritual lives in harmony are the too-often neglected building blocks of a strong marriage. The husband gets left behind in the spiritual race because he often spends his time doing other things that are not spiritually inclined rather than seeing to it that he fulfills his God-given role as the spiritual head of the home. He always has a valid reason for not going to church nor taking an active part in religious matters.

The second pitfall we must avoid is equally dangerous. Given our current cultural climate and especially the proliferation of "male-bashing" in the media and entertainment industries, it is too easy to forget about the importance of masculine leadership in or outside the home altogether. A good leader does not lord it over others. He leads by example and carries everyone along. He does not stand on a pedestal and make others feel they are not good enough. He is empathic and feels what others feel. A good leader knows that it is not about him but about those under and around him. He empowers those he leads and makes them feel treasured and loved. He is only happy when they are, and he can feel their pain as well as rejoice in their happiness.

In my opinion, the breakdown of many families today is due in a large part to the failure of men to assume their God-given responsibilities and with women not really knowing who they are in Christ Jesus. If, in order to avoid male domination, we swing to the other extreme and strip husbands of their authority, we will be disregarding God's plan for marriage and the family, and ultimately courting not only social but also spiritual disaster.

It is an overly pertinent matter that Peter attached an important personal application by indicating that the effectiveness of a husband's prayer life will be determined by the way he treats his wife. How else do you think a holy God would react when he witnesses a man who disrespects his wife kneeling before him and making requests? The Bible says in James 3:9–10:

> With the tongue we praise our Lord and Father, and with it we curse human beings, who have been made in God's likeness. Out of the same

mouth come praise and cursing. My brothers and sisters, this should not be.

God cannot work in confusion and has nothing to do with sin. He is not man that He would change his mind and be mocked! Whatever we sow, we reap! How do you expect to please him when you dishonour your spouse, then turn around to use that same mouth to praise God! You must understand that He is a holy God and nothing bad or evil can come near Him. He demands that you serve Him in spirit and in truth. If God permitted you to disrespect one another, being human, you would just throw caution to the winds and live life in abandonment. Despite this injunction from God, selfishness and entitlement are still rife in a relationship where God wants you to live in love, care, and compassion. You are children of God, yet you treat each other with levity and care little about the consequences.

Lean on Me

When contemplating marriage or when you get married, you are on a lifetime journey with your spouse. The Lord in His infinite wisdom saw that man alone without a companion was not going to make it. So, He made one for him; so that when he stumbled, she could lift him up. We can see this as stated in Ecclesiastes 4:9–12:

> Two are better than one, because they
> have a good return for their labor: If
> either of them falls down, one can
> help the other up. But pity anyone
> who falls and has no one to help them
> up. Also, if two lie down together,
> they will keep warm. But how can
> one keep warm alone? Though one
> may be overpowered, two can defend
> themselves. A cord of three strands is
> not quickly broken.

This applies to us in our spiritual lives too because couples are meant to edify, pray, and intercede for each other. When one is faltering and not walking the right way, the other is supposed to help. When faced with a challenge, they can team up together and fight, presenting a unified front. This is because it would be very easy to break one person but breaking two would be very difficult, especially if they are in unity.

In marriage, as I mentioned earlier, you are two different individuals with different ideologies, temperaments, upbringings, and so on, striving to become one. Because of this, sparks will fly; you will disagree on certain topics because both of you are wired differently. If you find out that you agree on everything in your lives, pause and think. The reason might be that one person has lost himself or herself and most times it is the less dominant spouse who compromises and loses herself to keep the peace. I am not trying to say disagreeing on some circumstances or situations should now be a defining quality in your lives. When you do disagree, it gives you the opportunity to listen and understand the other person's point of view. Sometimes it is impossible to believe that you can both have such different views concerning an issue and resolve these conflicts. You will disagree but work together toward the resolution of this conflict. I can say that unless you were cloned very carefully, it is impossible to agree on every subject. Come to think of it, when you find yourself having to settle and agree to everything all the time, even when it does not make sense, how do you feel? How do you carry on suppressing your feelings or reaction and believe that you will be happy and fulfilled? This would not augur well for your marriage as there will be a lack of authenticity and unity in the true sense of the word. It also shows that one of you is lording it over the other and this would result in the compliant or silent one feeling stifled and used. The relationship between you will not be balanced as only one person's ideas and feelings matter here.

You do not need a psychologist to tell you that your spouse is carrying a burden that is weighing her/him down. What do you do when you come to this realization? Do you offer to help alleviate this by sharing the weight, or do you feel that she/he should buckle up and try to do better? A loving spouse should demonstrate to the other that she/he is important by lending a helping hand when the other is weak or tired. It is not right to behave as if the chores are one person's responsibility alone. Remember that apart from Christ, she comes first in everything in your life because, on the scale of importance, she comes before your friends, business, your children, your parents, your house, your hobbies, or your Sunday morning catch-up on football. What I am trying to say here is that you and she/he are now inseparable. What hurts her should do the same to you! Need I remind you that you are one?

Remember your role as protector? This is when you bring it to action and start protecting her as reflected in the following words in Ephesians 5:28–29:

> In this same way, husbands ought to love their wives as their own bodies. He who loves his wife loves himself. After all, no one ever hated their own body, but they feed and care for it, just as Christ does the church.

Well, men, are you treating your spouses as you treat yourselves? Do you take into consideration what your wife's physical, emotional, and spiritual needs are?

Watch out, as sometimes no matter how tired some women are, they will continue going and going until they get all the work done. She may not say it but may be trying to do more than she is physically capable of doing. She wants to contribute her fair share toward the upkeep of the home. Husbands, do not forget that sometimes the demands of carrying children or caring for children and the whole family may be taking a toll on her and destroying her too. Society has made it such that she is not even spared from the criticisms or expectations of others. This may be mentally devastating and overwhelming for her. I once had a conversation with a woman who said she was very happy to be divorced from her husband. Put bluntly, she was ecstatic because her husband did everything within his power to demean, humiliate, and strip her of all self-esteem. He always not only told her but also made her feel she was not good enough nor capable. She was so gullible, defenceless, and naive, that she bought into this lie and started feeling inadequate and stupid. She said she could not do anything about this as she believed he was telling the truth about her. She finally got divorced and is now very happy. Husbands, be sensitive to your wives' needs as godly men and find ways to be proactive and try to prevent any possible scourge or dangers that may seek to tear them down. If you cannot help, seek help from family members or professionals who can do the job.

It cannot be a successful marriage if the spouses are selfish, insensitive, and entitled. For any marriage to succeed, both of you must note that there should be giving and receiving elements that must never be compromised. As friends, you should be able to always count on each other's support, love, and affection. Your wife should be aware that no matter the circumstances, she can share your burdens with laughter and above all be herself. No pretense is needed here. The questions then will be: Do you love her as Christ exemplified? Does true love flourish in your home? Is your home a Christian home where Christ is honoured? As a husband, are you willing to live in the strength of this love and direct the affairs of your home in wisdom? Have you resolved to become the best husband, the best father, and the best teacher in your home? When the need arises, will you readily sacrifice yourself and stand in your position as provider, protector, guide, and teacher to your children and all those under you? Do you honour your marriage by entirely helping each other to be the best you can be? Are you totally committed to your spouse?

Wives, are you willing to walk in the strength of God's love and be true to your calling and voluntarily and delightfully submit to the godly and wise leadership of your husband and fulfill all your functions as his helper? What about the children? Are you ready to raise them in the fear of the Lord? Will you work together with your spouse to build a home where Christ is revered, determine to dwell together, and enjoy each other, and faithfully join as helpers in everything that concerns your lives, working together in harmony to serve the Lord and your community and the whole world if called upon?

All these questions have just a few answers. This is all possible when you are filled with the Holy Spirit and you give Him authority over your lives so that He can begin to work in you and pour out into each one of you God's abundant love. As a result, you will then be able to fulfill your true calling in marriage.

Compatibility

When you meet for the first time and find out you are in love, compatibility is the last thing you think about. You bask in the euphoria of being in love. The last thing on your mind is the thought of the future. The notion here is that love alone is enough, and it is going to see you through! Because you are so in love, you just need to make it official and get married! You have all heard this several times being said by young lovers. This is where the problem begins. You cohabit and put up all pretense of being very kindhearted, well-mannered, considerate, and loving toward all. You are biding your time and waiting patiently for the question to be popped, then *bam!* Out goes the nice and in comes the real you!

We hear of children who have married and have decided to move away from parents for whatever reason. In most cases, this move is final. The parents wait in vain for even a call from them. The wait continues as days roll into weeks and weeks into months, and there is still no call from the children. Well, when the Bible says you leave your father and mother and cleave together, it does not mean to stop caring for them. We can see this clearly in the following passage: "Anyone who does not provide for their relatives, and especially for their own household, has denied the faith and is worse than an unbeliever" (1 Timothy 5:8). We can see here that this is not limited to only those of his own house but his own family, or a poor widow or relative who lives under his roof. It is mandatory to note here that the Christian religion strongly inculcates love and benevolence to all mankind and not adhering to this is contrary to what you stand for. So where does neglect of parents come into the equation? Why do you strive to separate yourself and stop caring for your family, parents, and siblings when you get married? I think there is a need for us to really go back to the Bible and find out what God requires of us—married or not! It is not uncommon to see aged parents relegated to the background withering away and yearning just to see or get a call from their children. I would like to say here that we truly reap what we sow. How would you feel if you found yourself old and abandoned?

What then is compatibility? According to the *Cambridge Dictionary,* it is "the fact of being able to exist, live, or work successfully with something or someone else." You might want to ask what this has to do with marriage! It is only necessary for you to take a step backward and a closer look at your beloved without the blinkers or the rose-tinted glasses. I am talking about a very careful look, not at the beauty but the inner qualities like faith, anger management, respect, and so on. Ask yourself who your spouse really is. This will reveal a lot of things to you. Then make your final decision as to whether he or she is the right spouse for you. When this is done, you will realize whether you would be able to exist, live, or work successfully with her/him or someone else. I have had some couples tell me that they think they will live together and get to know each other well for about two to three years before getting married. My question here is, do you really think this is enough time to know someone? What has the Bible got to say about this? Do not just jump into marriage; you do not need to cohabit to be sure of your choice either before you do.

A Compatibility Self-Test

A little game I like playing with people who are considering marriage goes like this: Close your eyes and empty your mind of all thought. Picture the person you are either engaged to or dating. Now, pretend you have a canvas in front of you and have suddenly become a great painter. Paint your partner's face as accurately as possible. Next, paint some wrinkles on their face, add some gray hair or make them bald and portray them with a very foul attitude. Imagine your courteous beloved as foul-tempered, mean-spirited, self-obsessed, and ungrateful with a rotund belly. Above all, give them a not-so-healthy appearance!

This is what happens when you marry; changes will take place all around you! What I try to show couples with this exercise is that most of them are in love with the idea of love. They have not considered the long-lasting effects of age, sickness, financial problems, and the vagaries of life creeping into their marriage. Are they willing to be each other's help?

I would like to mention here that the reason couples always think they are incompatible is that once they get married, they think their work is done. They believe they are now settled and have nothing more to work on. They had stumbled into this relationship and all the beautiful plans they had went out the window. Now they find out they have run out of their earlier zeal steam and momentum halfway through. They have no incentive and motivation to do all they had planned or imagined; they now just settle. The dissatisfaction now begins. They do not find any reason to work on themselves and bring about change. Need I say this is wrong because the work begins only after marriage.

As partners in a relationship, you must strive to make each other better. When embarking upon self-development and improvement, you must understand that as A tries to move ahead and make himself better, B should also be encouraged to follow suit and make herself better too. It does not need to be some great change but could be something like a hobby or that long-forgotten dream of pursuing further studies. If your financial position can permit you to do this. You can only change when you know what your needs and aspirations are. However, care should be taken not to demand change from your spouse as this is not very healthy nor helpful. You should be careful about this because if one improves and leaves the other behind, it will not be long before feelings of resentment start creeping into the relationship. As the less enterprising or dominant of you starts feeling dejected and unsatisfied! You find it difficult to even communicate about the simplest of things. As a result of this, you become indifferent and unsupportive towards each other. You find out you are suddenly unsupportive towards one another as you lack empathy and it suddenly feels better when one person is away. It is then not only the one left behind that would start feeling left behind and incompatible but both of you. Discontentment also creeps into the marriage and this is blamed on incompatibility. It is expedient for you to note that you are not incompatible unless you refuse to work on yourself and change. Note that you can change only yourself, not the other person. Lack of change in a relationship means a lack of progress. You are not going to remain the same; you will grow, and a lot will change about you.

I had a very beautiful and intelligent friend who got married and was blessed with a child. She was unable to shed the baby weight and remained slightly overweight. She said she started noticing subtle changes in her husband's behaviour. She saw nothing wrong in this as she was very confident that he still loved her. It was not long before the taunts began! He started calling her uncomplimentary names and even refused to go out with her as she was too fat and would shame him. Whenever she complained about his behaviour, she got abused physically and emotionally. It is not difficult to see what was happening here! What immaturity! Why do we become so selfish and self-centred that we begin to take each other for granted?

The joy of marriage cannot be underplayed. We were created for fellowship as human beings and when we come together as man and wife, committed to the same goals, and determined to make this union a success, nothing can come between us. The passage in Mark 10:9, "Therefore what God has joined together, let no one separate," is very apt here. God has united you and your spouse in marriage, and it is His desire that you build a long-lasting and trusting relationship. He wants you to build a fulfilling relationship with your spouse and to be present in your marriage. The union God envisioned for you was not one of selfishness where suddenly because you failed to work on you, you declare you want out! The reason: "Oh, we are not compatible anymore!"

It takes courage to be able to love someone amid all conceived faults and failures and to look each other in the face and express your displeasure without bias or guile. It also takes courage to be able and ready to face the ups and downs often encountered in life, cultivate the honesty to accept our mistakes, and move ahead to a higher ground of maturity and acceptance.

Communication is a two-way street; a great privilege God has bestowed on us as humans. We can choose to cherish this gift, or abuse it, use it to our detriment, and tear our partner apart. When we look around, most couples know nothing about one another's life. Some have little or no conversations other than how the kids are, rent, or groceries. They live like total strangers and each comes and goes as they please. Would it not be wonderful when you get into marriage to suddenly possess the superpowers to stay and build a very successful relationship with your spouse without communicating or making your feelings known? Does this sound like everyone's wish? It is not even remotely possible to do this! Even if you had a crystal ball or some magic mirror that could see into the inner recesses of someone's mind, it would be impossible to guess exactly what your spouse is feeling or thinking without the help of some form of communication. How do you agree if you do not communicate?

I have come to the realization that it is very easy to live lives without conflict! We just need to learn to communicate effectively. Without communication, it is almost impossible to get on the same page and keep your relationship working or vibrant and happy. How many of you reading this would sincerely say you prefer a relationship that is devoid of communication? When a relationship, especially marriage, begins to lack communication, it can quickly cause misunderstandings, resentments, and feelings of being physically and even emotionally far away or distant from each other—even if you are in the same room!

You must maintain effective communication in your marriage as this is one of the keys to a healthy relationship. The Bible has told us that God is love and, as a result, He wants us all to resolve our disagreements or issues with love. We have also learned that love is kind, peaceful, and gentle; it comes with a great deal of self-control. This is necessary as it is one of the elements of love that will enable you to communicate effectively with each other. As couples, when you let communication slip away from you and fall into the background of your relationship, don't you feel the distance that is created between the two of you? Why then do you not endeavour to make your partner feel like her feelings are not just because of the hormones raging or going out of whack in her body but that these matter to you as you think they are valid? This would make her understand that you are not only her spouse but her companion and that you value and care for her in the true sense of the word. The tension or mixed signals that have resulted in arguments and long stretches of silence and bitterness would be removed. Stop making each other feel as if you are walking on eggshells! When you have mastered this, you will ultimately achieve the healthy and loving relationship you seek.

During a marriage, some people become self-proclaimed kings and queens, lording it over each other! Some have just married for appearance's sake! When are you really going to grow up and do away with the pretense and hypocrisy? Just as you hurt, know that your partner hurts the same way or even more! You are not on opposite teams but are each other's cheerleader and strength! Do away with all falsehood and be yourself! If, for any reason, you cannot be authentic with your wife or husband, then there is a big problem. How then do you think you can agree and fight the devil who is here to steal, kill, and destroy? Why allow such misunderstanding to creep into your relationship? Why can you not resolve any differences between you two as soon as they crop up? Realize that the devil does not need a second invitation! He takes whatever crumbs you throw his way and works on them. He looks for any little crack in your relationship so that he can sneak in and make a place for himself in your lives. If you value your relationship or spouse, you will not let this happen; you will fight for what you love and treasure!

Every relationship, whatever the degree of compatibility as a couple, is a lot of work and effort and can survive only with willful and purposeful commitment to work on yourselves and the relationship. You, your partner, and your relationship will always be works in progress. Embrace that. You can't give someone everything all the time, nor can you expect it. You are both perpetually learning from each other and life, growing together and trying to give each other the best, also bringing out the best in the other person. The grass always seems greener on the other side. Stop comparing as the stakes keep getting higher and higher. Instead, just realize the value of what is in front of you. This doesn't mean you settle or compromise beyond your breaking point. Just learn to appreciate things for what they are rather than be deluded into a never-ending search for something better, spoiled by every iteration of "happily ever after" as depicted in the movies, glossy magazines, and books. Ever wondered what or when real life starts *after* the fairy-tale ending in the books and the movies? Due to the never-ending fear of the truth, even the writers do not want you disillusioned with a tale past this! Trust me, everyone wakes up to reality. Remember Snow White did after a long slumber, even if it was with a kiss!

Greater love has no one than this: to
lay down one's life for one's friends.

—John 15:13

Chapter Five

Love

When we talk about love, I am sure every one of us has an idea of what it is and what expectations we have of those who profess to love us. To some of us, love is the mushy, knee-jerking and mind-boggling, breathless feeling we experience when we meet someone we care for. Some would vouch that this is not a very easy road to take. Love is exhilarating and is meant to be enjoyed. We have seen love according to human perception splashed on billboards, television screens, and all through pages of romantic novels. Love here is a feeling or an emotion that can sometimes be used to get what we want, then turned off and on according to our whims and caprices. Love has become so cheapened selfish and deceitful, that it has lost its appeal. This is when love is not enough because love is a choice we make and not just another mushy feeling. It is both enduring, longsuffering and caring.

Throughout the pages of the Bible, love is not a feeling but exemplified as a conscious choice—something we intentionally choose to do for those we love. An example is Jesus Christ's choice to be a ransom for our sins by dying on the cross. This is not a love that overtakes us, rendering us helpless and incapable of thought as we forget ourselves! Most couples believe that love is just a feeling, which can appear magically and disappear when they no longer need it or when the novelty has worn off! For some, it takes a tragedy for them to suddenly realize they need to profess their undying love or at least start acting in a more loving, caring, and understanding way toward their partner, while others feel that their love should swing from one person to another like a pendulum or a monkey swinging from branch to branch.

The kind of love I am talking about is not like that mentioned above. It is love in its purest form as explained in 1 Corinthians 13:4–8:

> Love is patient, love is kind. It does not envy, it does not boast, it is not proud. It is not rude, it is not self-seeking, it is not easily angered, it keeps no record of wrongs. Love does not delight in evil but rejoices with the truth. It always protects, always trusts, always hopes, always perseveres. Love never fails.

It is not the warm fuzzy feeling you experience. This love is long-lasting and can stand the test of time. It is a love where you are not afraid to be vulnerable in the face of it. As the Bible says, it never fails. It is reflective of the love the Lord God has for His people and should be seen in the love the committed husband has for his wife.

"I love you" are the three easiest and most magical words you can use to express how you feel about someone you care for or your spouse. When you look at these words in the context of 1 Corinthians 13, be careful how loosely you use them. Realize that these words are not to be thrown around casually as they hold great meaning and demand that they are said in all honesty, and sincerely meaning every word. Be ready to understand that when used, you must understand the import of what you are saying and be determined to break them down and state boldly that, when you say you love someone, you are saying:

I am patient and kind to you.

- I do not envy you.
- I do not boast in front of you.
- I am not proud before you.
- I am not rude to you.
- I seek your good and not my own.
- I am not easily angered by you.
- I keep no record of your wrongs.
- I am ready to lay down my life for you.

Can we really practice this exemplary love shown to us by Christ and love like this all the time? When the above factors are put into consideration, it brings us to the love of our Savior. So, what love has the potential to keep us going? Is it when as couples, you make a conscious effort to put your partner's negative qualities aside and focus on his positives? I am sure there is much more we need to do!

In all ramifications, to love and be loved is just wonderful and must be treasured! *Love* is a wonderful word in itself! It evokes in us different feelings! It is not only wonderful but exhilarating and fulfilling. It is what marriage is and encompasses! It is so heartwarming! God commands the husband to love his wife just as Christ loves the church in Ephesians 5:28, 33. Clearly, God's instruction to the husband to love his wife just as he loves himself is the benchmark of marriage. In a world that is filled with self-centeredness and entitlement, are husbands living up to their calling? Do they know the meaning of this self-giving love? When we take a quick look at how Christ loved the church, it does not take long for us to realize that the love a husband expresses or shows his wife pales in comparison.

How then does Christ love the church? Ephesians 3:18–19 says the love of God passes knowledge. It is so broad that you cannot get around it, especially without a relationship with Christ, and too deep that it is all-encompassing. Christ's love is so wide and tall that throughout eternity, we will continue to learn of this amazing love. Not even the greatest theologians would be able to explain it to the fullest. The Bible in Romans 5:8, however, states that Jesus's love, as exemplified for us, is first and foremost an unconditional free love. By this, it means that the person doing or giving this love does not require anything to be done by other people in exchange for it. It does not have conditions attached to it. The beauty of this is that this love liberates. You do not have to be a certain way, act a certain way, be a certain colour, or belong to a certain race to deserve or be loved this way.

This love is not forced but it is volitional, in that God chooses to love us as seen in Deuteronomy 7:7: "The LORD did not set his affection on you and choose you because you were more numerous than other peoples, for you were the fewest of all peoples." Or in Ephesians 1:6–7:

> To the praise of his glorious grace,
> which he has freely given us in the One
> he loves. In him we have redemption
> through his blood, the forgiveness of
> sins, in accordance with the riches of
> God's grace.

In practicing this love, there is no coercion nor force of any kind. You love because you have chosen to do so not because Mr. A is watching or doing the same. The greatest truth is that, like all things done under duress, when you love because you are forced to or you are trying to please someone, it is never successful. Let us shed the pretense and love like Jesus did and still does. He did not hold back! He gave it all and died on the cross for us.

This is a huge challenge. How do we go about achieving this? I am sure, as you look at it, you are beginning to even doubt whether you are capable of this type of love. You must be asking yourself if you have missed something in this ideology of love. You cannot even fathom the possibility of loving another this way! Your selfish nature immediately raises its ugly head and you ask why you must love like this. What is the guarantee that your spouse will reciprocate this big sacrifice you are expected to make? This reaction is normal because self-preservation is a very distinguishable attribute of our carnal nature. It is far easier for us to think about ourselves and our needs rather than the needs of those around us, no matter how much we profess to love someone! When we live life in this way, it is only beneficial for us. It is not difficult for our spouse to fathom that we do not truly love them as our attitude depicts this easily. Note, however, that if God has shown that it is possible, it surely is.

The Bible says in Psalm 37:5, "Commit your ways to the Lord; trust in Him and He will do it." The idea is that if you have a wife, or if you find it difficult loving your spouse like Christ loved His church, just commit yourself, your relationship, to the Lord and

He will do it for you. He will show you how to love and give of yourself better.

We cannot let ourselves be vulnerable enough to love fearlessly as the Bible enjoins us to do. This is very easy to see by all and is especially true with regard to our spouses. One of the primary characteristics of godly love is that it is sacrificial. Let me invite you to take a closer look at verse 5. What is it really talking about? It says that love is "not self-seeking." This means that this love we possess should be focused more upon others than ourselves, to follow and reinforce what the Bible says: "Greater love has no one than this: that he lay down his life for his friends" (John 15:13). Of course, this is exactly the type of love that Jesus boldly and lovingly exemplified for us! He loved us so much that He did not think about Himself but became sin and died in our place so that we did not have to die, and so that we could also show this type of love to others especially to our spouses. As mere mortals, can we learn to love like this in our marriage?

Because we are not able to love anyone, not even our wife as God wants us to love her, for this perfect love to begin to emanate and flow through us, the only choice we have is to invite and surrender all control to the Holy Spirit. We can then carry out His works within us by putting to death our selfishness, entitlement, infirmities, distractions, and all other things that act as potential hindrances to our lives and marriages. The love God showed for his people that we are to emulate must be about the other person, not us. As we love them, we must also be conscious of the fact that we must be willing to meet their needs if we are in a position to do so.

Philippians 2:4 states "not looking to your own interests but each of you to the interests of the others," instructing us that love means being willing to put the interests of others (your spouse) first by laying aside your own personal interests.

I feel at this stage, you are beginning to feel very dissatisfied! However, it is not my intention to make you feel inadequate in any way as it is very clear that, as humans, we have not explored nor gotten close to expressing that kind of unconditional and sacrificial love to our spouses nor others in our lives as enjoined in the Bible! I am sure the questions on your mind are: "How is this even possible? We are not God to start with. How are we going to bridge this gap and love like God?"

Do not be discouraged. Trust me when I say God knows that we are only mere mortals full of selfishness and guile, and this form of love is nearly impossible for our carnal nature and would not come naturally to us as we are incapable of reproducing it by our own strength. That is why He made a way out for us to be able to love our spouses in a way that would please and glorify Him.

Bear in mind that we did not become Christians by merit but because of the redemptive work of Christ on the cross. Left to our own devices, we would have perished! Christ came and died for us. With the help of the Holy Spirit, Christ is willing to continue to great and mighty things—in us, through us, with us, and for us—that we cannot even comprehend. Thus, Jesus is fully able to empower us as His children as we see in these words from John 13:34 stating, "A new command I give you: Love one another. As I have loved you..." There is nothing else we must do but surrender everything to Him. He will fulfill His promise. If God created the institution of marriage, He knows how to preserve it.

Can husbands now begin to imitate Christ's selfless love, as seen in Ephesians 5:25, where they are commanded to follow Jesus's example as they seek to love their wives? It's a manifested love—Jesus showed us His love in words and deeds. There was no pretense, ego, or guile. He not only declared to us that He loved us but displayed and proved it by dying on the cross for us, and He still tells us He loves us now through His Spirit in us and what He does for us. He shows us He loves us. He protects us from the devices of the evil one, prays for us, guards us, strengthens us, helps us, defends us, teaches us, comforts us, chastens us, equips us, empathizes with us, and provides for all our needs best of all; there are no conditions attached. It is a pure and selfless love devoid of any guile or malice. It would not be love if it were not expressed! How else would we know what He feels for us? So, the Bible in Hebrews 4:14–16 says, "Love does not long exist without expression."

A Godly husband is to use these standards to judge his relationship with his wife. It is no mean feat for a man to love his wife to this extent. It is, however, not impossible for a husband to strive toward this goal to fully love his wife in that way or to that extent either. With this model in mind, a husband could try to love his wife as enjoined by the Bible.

Loving like this would be nearly impossible if we did not seek help from the Lord and get to know Jesus more intimately. Can our desire to know Jesus just be wished into being? Or can we just go through the motions and become more loving toward our spouses? No, this cannot happen by fluke. It is only possible if we establish good fellowship with other Christians, read God's Word, and pray earnestly for this ability. As mentioned earlier, this cannot be wished into being as it would take time and continuous fellowship and persistent prayer. We can only begin to love like Jesus through the Holy Spirit when we seek God and depend on Him to help us in all aspects of our lives.

We Fail at Self-Giving Love

A Godly marriage is one in which you resolve to remove all pettiness and sense of self-aggrandizement and consciously replace these with forbearance, loving patience, and grace. This will be reflected in the way you treat one another, especially when handling conflict and other pressures of life. It goes a long way in reflecting your love for the Lord and what drives you. As a couple, you are to serve each other lovingly without any bias, malice, nor guile. This is made explicit in Ephesians 5:25, where the Bible tells us we are no longer separate individuals when we get married—we are one!

Most of us have a notion of what we can tolerate from our spouses and what we cannot. I once heard a guy tell another that "he must be a man and learn to control his wife"; after all, he was the husband! This left a very bitter taste in my mouth as I began to wonder what made him think it was his responsibility to control his wife. Had she suddenly become a wayward animal that needed to be controlled or reined in?

Our friends are full of the greatest wisdom that they can reel out; what they consider fair and manly and what they or you should not tolerate. They are so good at giving unsolicited advice that is meant to work for you, such as: "You should show her that you are a man" or "Be a man!" and so on. Remember Proverbs 1 says, "Blessed is the man who does not sit in the counsel of the ungodly." If these friends had a little concept or knowledge of God, they would not be peddling such advice! We forget that the passage in Ephesians 5:25 states, "Husbands, love your wives, just as Christ loved the church and gave himself up for her."

Are you doing exactly this when you indulge in such idle talk? Who nominated your friends as counsellors? There are no exceptions; God wants you to love your wife and that is it! You can take your spouse's behaviour that could be construed as negative in a godlier way and not give the perfect response as we are often tempted to do. Seeing past this behaviour and determining to love her just the same is wonderful. Biting your tongue in this situation or channelling your interaction in a godlier way for your spouse's good and for God's glory, even if this makes you feel like a loser at that moment, will stave off quarrels until you can discuss it calmly. Knowing that the glory will go to God is well worth it.

Most of us show love only when we are in the company of others! Stop! Why put up appearances to please others instead of being true to yourself? Remember that it takes too much effort to pretend. Just be yourself. Stop chasing shadows and trying to please people! You are only cheating yourself of the blessings God intends for you. If you know what the problem is with your marriage, fix it! Build your marriage on a solid foundation—Christ with whom you never need to be anything but yourself! Just because you're married does not mean you can treat your spouse in any way you please. A whiny, callous, and mean man is as unattractive as a desperate needy and clingy woman. You are in a relationship as equals and have the responsibility of each other as a priority, so it is inappropriate for one partner to Lord it over the other. This is not only very wrong but inappropriate too. You are trying to please people so that they think you are brave! The Bible warns against this and says in Matthew 10:28, "Do not be afraid of those who kill the body but cannot kill the soul. Rather, be afraid of the One who can destroy both soul and body in hell." You have nothing to fear from man. Your life is not dependent on their approval.

God sees you even when you are in the dark, and He is the only one you should seek to please, not man. So why can you not express your love to your spouse even when you are not in the full glare of people? Whatever is hindering your expression of love for each other, work on it together and build a better relationship. Like I said before, you will do better as a team! It is time to forget your individual idiosyncrasies and work for the betterment of your relationship. You are in it together and for life! Whatever you do, just remember that God would never ask you to do something that you are incapable of doing nor what has the potential to hurt you. We are not just meant to be show-offs but to practice true, undying, and perfect love with each other.

Relationships have become so unimportant that some of you will just be in a relationship, not because you really want to be with that person. You want to do it because your friends are all doing it and, after all, you need to show them that you are as good as they are! You want to show you can handle a marriage just as well as they can, and you could do just okay if not better with some company. In times like this, you forget to think. You just do whatever you want to do without considering the consequences. Marriage is a serious business and must never be trivialized.

Competition and envy can becloud your judgment. You can become so impatient with yourself that you question your self-worth and just dive into any relationship that comes your way. You try your best to see that the relationship ends in a marriage even though you know that you are not ready for it. I have heard some even blaming God for not providing a partner for them so they could get married! They are not waiting for the right person.

Note here that it is truly unfair for both of you to be stuck in a relationship just for the sake of being in one. It will not take long before you suddenly realize that you would rather be doing anything but stay married. It's little wonder you feel very overwhelmed and boxed in. You are now so impatient with everything that you become frustrated with how things are going in your life. Our God meant business when he instituted marriage! It was not to be taken as a challenge but was meant to last a lifetime. We were to treat it with reverence, love, and respect. You only need to be patient and wait for God's plans for you to be unveiled because He knows better, and what He has planned for you is way better than what you have planned for yourself. Drop this idea of living up to other's expectations! Be authentic, be you, for you are more than enough. Marriage or being married is not what really defines you but who you really are in Christ Jesus.

Our Misconception of the Importance of Marriage

When we fail to recognize marriage as a calling and a very important aspect of our lives, we belittle it. Culturally, it becomes a hobby or something nice to do "if you're into that kind of thing." To put it bluntly, we just do it because we have seen others doing it! Sometimes it becomes just an obligation, a chore, or a prerequisite that says, loudly enough for anyone willing to hear, that you have finally arrived at your destination. It certainly isn't worth any sacrifice, and you certainly do not think it is something you would sacrifice your individuality or career for—not the least put yourself out for! We live in a society that tells us in no uncertain terms that everything trumps marriage. Our career goals, education, travel plans, and every other thing we would want to do can take precedence. There's no hurry. We can cross the marriage bridge when we get to it. If you are a woman and you deem it necessary to give up your career and become a housewife, you are treated with disdain because you have no economic leverage to compete with your colleagues. You would think the man you gave this up all for would be more understanding and accord you some respect! Instead, you find out that he has suddenly become too busy and hardly has the time of day for you. Sometimes you are treated like some highly prized jewel or a piece of furniture and at other times, he wants to lord it over you and make you feel like a shrimp that should beg and grovel for every penny she needs. There are no guarantees that after the grovelling, you will be given what you need. You are reminded constantly and indirectly of how little you contribute to the well-being of the family! Excuse me here, but can we quantify in monetary terms the contribution of a full-time wife, mother of your children cum babysitter? If we were to hire a full-time maid, what would be the salary? Would she be with you around the clock, share your woes, clean, cook, and raise your children for you without a salary? Would she stand your excesses and nurse you when you are sick?

It is high time we started respecting each other in marriage. Appreciation is in short supply, and we take each other for granted! We have become so entitled and self-centred that this has transcended into our homes. The spouse who works feels that is his contribution to the relationship! He can hardly spare enough time to do other things with his spouse. After all, he has been slogging all day and as a result, he is free to do whatever he wants to do. He can even decide to stay out all night or trudge in late at night because he has had to put in so many hours working for the good of his family. His thinking is that the spouse at home has just been sitting idle and twiddling her thumbs. After all, what is housework?

The funniest part here is that this spouse expects a great marriage, an unbeatable cordon bleu chef/cook, great sex, and a very happy family. He/she has no right to expect anything else but continue serving her partner. He reserves the right to come and go as he pleases. No questions asked! While this picture is the norm in most homes, it reminds me of a master and servant's relationship—not a marriage between two equal beings!

If marriage is a calling and equivalent to a career or vocation, that means it is your life's work and it is something to be treasured because when you lose it, you will be on the streets; it's not a job and not something you do on the side. You do not decide to be married when you are drunk. This decision requires determination, conscious thought, and choice. It takes precedence over everything you do. It requires patience, and you must build the rest of your life around it. It is not an afterthought nor something you try to fit in later when you have saved up enough money, enjoyed life, and accomplished "more important" things. Do not get married if you are not ready for it! The world has witnessed too many failed marriages, shattered lives, and brokenness.

The saddest part is that this has a long-lasting impact as it negatively affects a lot of innocent people who desperately want to get married as they become confused and reluctant after witnessing the failed institution of marriage. They are in no hurry to find their spouse, get married, begin a lifelong commitment, and practice self-giving love.

The result is that when people get married late, there is less likelihood that they will meet their spouses when both are ready to make a commitment, and there are fewer marriage–ready men and women in the dating pool even for those who are looking seriously for a spouse. They then just settle for the next available prospect.

However, all hope is not lost! We serve a God who is awesome and forgiving. God is greater than any trouble that may seek to derail us from the path of marriage, and He works with what we give Him. All of us, married, single, divorced, widowed, dating, or alone, can pray every day for the grace we need to live out Christ's call to perfection in an imperfect world.

It is time to rise and take the reins of marriage back from the devil and really practice self-giving love and support the institution of marriage. Let us make it our responsibility to pray for each other, whether married or not. Let us encourage one another through the way we live our lives by exemplifying the type of love Jesus showed us. We must be considerate of one another.

We know that in all things God works for the good of those who love Him, who have been called according to his purpose.

—Romans 8:28

Chapter Six

The Power of Positivity

We live in a world where we have become so self-indulgent and entitled. Things must just be the way you want them, or you feel you have lost everything as it has to be all about you and no one else. Your spouse must do everything to make sure you are happy; if not, he becomes the worst human being you have ever met! You begin to wonder what drove you into marrying such a person. You blame your luck or whatever your belief allows. May I remind you here that marriage is a very beautiful thing; I bet you thought so too when you got married, and the Bible says, "He who finds a wife, finds what is good and receives favor from God" (Proverbs 8:22). Well, you must accept that this statement might seem a little bigger than we can even comprehend if we are not living our lives to glorify God. Why would the Bible say this if marriages were so difficult? How do you make sure you do not lose this thought? You must be careful not to let negativity into your lives. I cannot emphasize enough the power of positivity in any relationship. Being negative is another way of saying you lack the faith to see the relationship through or that your spouse is not worth fighting for. Make a conscious effort to reflect more on your partner's positive qualities. Minimize the time you spend reflecting on his negative qualities as this will always open a door to discovering many of such qualities that will only infuriate you.

A marriage does not work in a day. It is a journey of a lifetime that involves you, your spouse, and God. If one of you falls, invariably both of you have fallen. You are each other's greatest support because successful marriages do not just happen coincidentally; they are only possible when spouses purposely work hard and commit to creating a loving and positive home where there is love and above all, each person is valued and validated.

One of the most important things you should do is have positive thinking concerning your marriage. Paying attention to your thoughts before speaking sometimes is challenging, but when practiced facilitates more positive conversations between you and your spouse. If you cultivate a positive attitude toward your spouse, you will not only be more honest, closer, and loving, but your relationship will become more nurturing and nourishing. Both of you will feel loved and appreciated. If one person is not around, you will feel like you cannot wait for him to be back; you will feel like seeing him/her immediately. You will miss his/her company and will begin sending little surprise messages to each other. You will not be able to wait for the day to end so you can be together. This is not magic. It is the power of transparency. Some of us spend our days wondering where and what our spouses are up to! We check their phones, emails, chats, etc. just to make sure they are not cheating on us. Before you got to this point, you had already decided not to trust him maybe because of past incidences that you had witnessed. This did not just happen overnight; you had resolved or determined in your heart not to trust! Be aware that these unpleasant incidences may or may not have happened to you. However, you have conveniently tucked these in a very safe place and resolved never to allow yourself to fall into the same trap. Realize that before you have a lack of trust in your heart, you made a conscious choice to let it fester.

As I stated earlier, be conscious of your thought processes, pay more attention to your thoughts, and strive to replace the negative ones with positive ones. How about instead of thinking your spouse is cheating on you, channel your thoughts to more productive things? The Bible has this to say about it in Proverbs 23:7: "As a man thinks in his heart, so he is." I have heard so many people say it is easier said than done as they make excuses for their negative attitude. Some make up stories to support the way they feel. This is not limited to unbelievers; it is very common among believers too.

The key to success here is to communicate cheerfully, sincerely, and positively with your spouse. God wants all of you, and He knows the best remedy for the ills you are going through. We only just need to let Him in on our problems and He will make everything right. No matter how hard we try in this world, we can never be perfect because the Bible says none of us are perfect; we are just striving for perfection and when that happens, we will no longer be on Earth because Earth is not for the perfect. We find ourselves struggling in our marriages because we have left out the most important part of our lives: our senior partner, God. In Psalm 127:1–5, the Bible says, "Unless the LORD builds the house, the builders labor in vain. Unless the LORD watches over the city, the guards stand watch in vain." There is the DIY (do-it-yourself) mentality that is prevalent in our culture and it is taken into homes, not only for furniture but for our marriages too. Once you are married, you forget the Lord and decide to do it yourself. After all, your dreams, goals, ambitions and, above all, marriage are simple things and they can be done by you. You have seen how easy this is in television shows! You leave God out of it. When will it become clear to you that God does not want just some parts of you, but all of you? He is interested in even the minutest thing that concerns you. After all, He created you for fellowship with Him. It takes three to form a successful marriage: a man and woman who love each other, and the greatest partner of all—God! We must fear the Lord, revere Him by worshipping Him and obeying His Word!

With a resolution to make it work, we must focus on our spouse's good qualities. The more you focus on their bad attitude or qualities that irritate you, the more you begin to see the bad attributes become more and more pronounced and magnified beyond bounds. This has the ability to steal your peace. Instead, why not make a conscious effort to notice all the little things your spouse does that you just love and express appreciation for those things? It helps a lot if you let your spouse know what you love about him. You must not try to manipulate, coerce, or punish your spouse. Success in marriage is not just a myth; it is a project that both spouses must undertake to work on wholeheartedly, happily, and together.

A positive attitude will not just drop onto your head nor your lap so you can put it on like a cap! This, as with anything good, demands that you put great effort into it, cultivate it and nurture it. It would not be enough if I said every married person must put in 50 percent in their marriages as this would not work. It demands 100 percent from both partners and nothing else. Love one another and try not to deny each other the benefit of being yourselves and living your lives to the fullest. Note that if this relationship is going to work, it will not be about a single person as it concerns both of you. Maintain a deep focus on

God believing that your spouse will turn out to be the woman or man God intended her or him to be, and your marriage will be as God wanted it.

You and your spouse must be determined to maintain healthy and active lifestyles as it is very difficult to be stress-free and positive when you are going through a lot of health-related problems. You must strive to live or adopt healthy lifestyles and support each other throughout. I have clients who come to me and say their spouse is not supportive, and they have been trying to lose weight on their own to no avail. They say the reason they cannot lose weight is that their overweight spouse sees no need in this and does not encourage them. The clients talk about wanting to lose weight but are not willing to do anything about it. My advice here is that if weight is the problem, then make a commitment with your spouse to improve your diet, eat healthily, and exercise together. The support and time you spend together will strengthen your marriage and bring you two closer.

As a couple, you must pick your friends wisely. Surround yourselves with positive-minded people. As a child, my father always said this to us: "Show me your friends and I will tell you what you are." I do not need to mention here how irritated I felt when he said this. My thinking then was that I was obviously not the same as my friends and would never be. Truth be told, the friends or company you choose can affect your life in a very important way. This is because they are not just friends but your support system, and if they are not positive-minded, the counsel you get from them cannot be positive either. You might wonder what this has to do with positivity in marriage—a lot, if I must say, as its importance cannot be overemphasized. I will try to explain why as much as I can.

My longtime friend got married to her beau and they were very happy together. Then her husband changed jobs and brought home some new colleagues. They soon became her friends too and their visits were quite frequent. They talked about almost everything and it was not long before she realized they did not value relationships and had little or no respect for women. Their lives revolved around them—the guys only—as they spared no thought for their spouses. They were, however, supposedly Christians!

She was quick to realize that things started changing in the home. Her husband's thinking changed; he suddenly started making condescending statements that were in line with what the friends did and thought. They did not believe that working women could be trusted and would never want their wives to do so. She discovered that she and her husband started disagreeing a lot over trivial matters, issues that never mattered in their relationship. This continued for a while, and it was beginning to put a strain on their marriage. Finally, they sought the face of the Lord and opted for Christian counselling. God restored their marriage and opened her husband's eyes to see that their marriage was almost destroyed because of the unequal yoking by the "friends."

A good question or point to be noted here is that though the friends were "Christians," did they really know God? Were they walking in the precepts and knowledge of the Almighty? She confessed that staying positive had become extremely difficult and nearly impossible when they were surrounded by negative friends. She also said her mood, disposition, and how she dealt with situations had been affected too. She could not seem to manage as well as she did prior to this. Her greatest ability now is that she has learned how to smile again. She has discovered that her mood just lightens up and all stress is relieved. She further says she now celebrates with her husband for everything, big or small! She seizes every opportunity to be thankful to God for her spouse; she even tells him how grateful she is for him and he does the same. The results have been very astounding! They are happier, more positive, and appreciate one another. This is what I refer to as purposeful and intentional gratitude. This is a wonderful way to get you both focused on what is beautiful and good in your marriage and each other.

Just Be Yourself

You are one of a kind, an original, a masterpiece. Travel from one end of the world to the other and you would not see another you. God has made you and bestowed upon you a very distinct and special identity. This cannot be taken from you unless you choose not to honour it and let it lie dormant. You are uniquely made by God. You do not have to live up to the Joneses! God has created you for a relationship with Himself and others; we can see this stated in Jeremiah 1:5: "Before I formed you in the womb, I knew you, before you were born, I set you apart; I appointed you as a prophet to the nations." Rejoice in this knowledge for nothing can beat the fact that your heavenly Father knows you intimately and wants to establish a relationship with you. It does not end there; He wants you to live to your full potential and be what He has designed you to be, not a copy of another person or character so that you can relate fully with him and with others without any manmade restrictions. Revel in this and embrace who you are! You are peculiar and special. A masterpiece! Just be you and you will be able to find happiness in the small things in life. There are no guarantees in life, so what we have is just the now. Embrace this.

Why waste your time and energy trying to be what or who you are not? Bear in mind that when you cannot be yourself, your heart and mind are divided, with confusion assaulting and attacking you from all angles. Most of the time you are lost as you cannot tell the part you are supposed to play. In college, a not-so-young roommate of mine, whom for the purpose of this story I'll call Claire, found herself amid people who were a little younger than her and hailed from wealthy families. To fit in with this crowd, she always wanted to project an air of affluence. She tried dressing a certain way and changed the way she normally spoke when in the company of the people she wanted to impress. Her quest to be accepted, however, was futile. Unbeknownst to her, they mimicked her voice, mocked her in her absence, and called her pretentious and fake.

You see, everyone saw through Claire's facade! Pretending to be somebody else did not make her feel any better nor did it make her more likeable. Instead, it created avenues for people to mock, belittle, and insult her. Claire became frustrated as she was in a fix and, as a result, could not really be herself. She had lost her real self as she failed to be authentic and true. The crowd she craved to belong to ignored her and treated her with disdain as they knew no better. Sadly, she started failing in her studies. Claire could not graduate from college as she got rusticated. She had failed and unfortunately had to leave school. Claire failed to realize that she could never be those she tried so hard to be. In the process, too, she forgot to strive to be the best she could be. She gave in to the devil's distraction and failed in being all God had created her to be.

If, for any reason, you have been trying to be somebody else, *stop*, and note that there is no time like now for you to stand tall, reassess your priorities, and take your God-given place in society. God spared nothing while creating you. Give of yourself in good works and life because God has made and equipped you with so much so that you can bring about a positive change in people's lives. You are complete just as you are, and your spouse married you for a reason; in trying to change this, you might lose yourself in the process. Do not cheat yourself by trying to be what you were not created to be as trying to do this will end up hurting you more. The heart is a very fertile ground and you reap what you sow. You will be torn apart in all directions trying to fill a need only the Lord can fill. Your happiness will flee and leave you bitter and dissatisfied, making people scared of any interaction with you. There is nothing as uninspiring as a pretentious person. This will have a negative impact on your marriage and family life. So be yourself and embrace your God-given potentials. God has a special ministry assigned just for you, and no one can change this, nor take it away from you!

I have heard many couples say that their spouse, husband or wife, was not like that before they got married. So, what changed? You know the surprising thing? It might be that you were driven or made to become this way due to circumstances or maybe the change came about because you felt inadequate, that you were not good enough for your spouse. You thought you needed to be different or like the girl or boy next door to keep him or her attracted to you! When will you realize that you are you and you are not married to the man or woman next door and neither is your spouse! When I say change starts with you, it does not mean you should strip yourself of your God-given attributes and character and try to become someone else. These qualities are what make you beautiful and special. When God created you, He had a blueprint just made for you. You are no one's clone nor copy! You are special and loved by God! Your attributes speak of your individuality and uniqueness. You should only try to correct things that do not enhance these God-given traits. Do not try thwarting the maker's design and creativity!

If you are not educated and you feel the need for this, go ahead and get an education. If you need a skill you do not possess, get trained on it if need be. Do not try to be another person and blame an outside influence for the drastic change in character or attitude and tastes. This is not so and will not work well for you. Your attempt at trying to be perfect will be futile as you are no longer the person you used to be; God made you just perfect the way you are.

Let us assume that someone wants to marry you and is trying to get to know you, but you try to be someone else; they will be left confused as your real self is hidden somewhere and only a facade is presented to them. You reveal what you think they want to see. It is like being on the one-hundredth date and still not knowing anything nor making any headway in the relationship. The result? There will be no success in the union. Quit the role-playing and be yourself! This makes perfect sense because for how long are you going to continue being fake, stifling your individuality while trying to be what you are not? You thought pretending to be what you were not and in the process losing your individuality and everything you stood for so as to fit in was the right way to go after all; You just needed to get married and this is the only way to make your spouse love you desperately and your life will just be perfect. Have you ever wondered how long this would last? For how long would you have to carry on with this façade before your real self actually emerges? What would be your spouse's reaction then? Is he going to love the real you? When you find it necessary to pretend to be what you are not, why not go back to the creator who made you in His image and declared that you were "good". You have no reason to force yourself into a relationship with someone who makes you feel less than you are, incapable, not good enough, resulting in a low self-concept and you trying to be someone different just so you can have a ring on your finger! Listen! God made you more than enough and endowed you with all good attributes to see you through life. You do not need validation from someone to live a good life.

Note that when you have tried every form of manipulation and blackmail and realized that you are a shadow of whom you were initially, you have not only become too available but uninteresting. Your spouse cannot find the individuality or personality that attracted him to you as it has been lost somewhere along the way.

You gave too much, and in the process, you lost yourself. You are now a very poor reflection of who you were! My question here is: Do you love this new you? Are you happy with what you have become? Stop before it is too late for you are your greatest cheerleader!

Remember, your spouse should be the one to know you more than any other person and love you for who you are. If you do the math correctly, you are bound to spend most of your life with them. If you base your marital success on another person's success, you are heading for misery and failure because you will find that the stakes keep getting higher and higher as you can never seem to match up. During this time, you will forget the dreams you had for your marriage, bitterness will creep in, and at the end of it all, you will not be able to give your all to the relationship. Your decisions and choices will revolve around another as you will not be thinking about being you and this will determine the outcome. You will find out you will never be satisfied because the grass will always be greener on the other side. This will make you feel smaller and smaller! You will be placed in a position where anything that is done for you will fall short and it will become difficult for you to be pleased or thankful. Your dreams will be easily shattered, as you have been trying to live another person's life.

There are no killers of joy as deadly as competition and comparison, and no poison as potent as envy.

So beware, do not compare yourself, your gifts, or any other attribute God has bestowed upon you to anyone. This is a trap you never want to fall into because you will never be contented, and your joy will never be full. Look up to God and let Him reveal His plans for you, who you really are in Him, and what your true worth is.

Permit me to say here that every woman has a vision of what she is or wants to be. She has her dreams and ambitions. She knows what she sees of herself, where she has been, and when she gets involved in a relationship with a man, she envisions herself in that relationship and dreams about a brilliant future and life with her spouse. She seeks security, love, respect, and permanence. The man becomes a promise to her. She helps him fulfill the promise and he does the same for her. They should work hand in hand to fulfill each other's vision—and this then becomes their collective vision as it fits perfectly into their lives. They do not have dreams that take them far away from their common goal.

Be reminded that you are enough. You're plenty. God has made you just the way He intended you to be. The Bible says in Psalm 139:14–15: "I praise you because I am fearfully and wonderfully made; your works are wonderful, I know that full well." Why then are you wasting your life and time away? You do not need anybody's approval or affirmation to live as God intended you to! Go ahead and enjoy your fellowship with God and your spouse! Now you know that there are not two of you nor are you counterfeit or fake! Grasp this if nothing else. Make the best of your life. No one can replace you! There is no photocopy of you. You are unique in your own way and that makes you more than enough. Realize you are living beneath your calling and make a mess for yourself when you try to compete or change yourself to be someone else or fit into an ideal of perfection for someone else. If along the line, you find out that your spouse intends for you to change and be like someone else, then there is a problem. There is a much more important aspect of having the perfect spouse and that is you. You deserve the best and that is the right to be the person God created you to be! You do not have to act in a certain way or be another person's clone to meet any man or woman's approval. In fact, God has made the right person for you who is bound to be as crazy about you as you are about him! He/she should love all of your flaws or no flaws and let you be you! You come in a package! A real man or woman will love you no matter what.

All you can do is work on being the best you can be of yourself. Rest assured when I say you will never be perfect because we are all imperfect beings, but you can work on refining who you are, or addressing your insecurities so that healing and restoration from your old wounds and hurts can be resolved. The only person you can change on this journey is you because that is all you have control over. Make sure you are not changing to satisfy another person; if you do, you will become that person's creation rather than who God made you to be, and there is no way you are going to be happy.

Some old friends of ours came to live with us for some months while they looked around for something to do. I was surprised to see that the extroverted and friendly girl we knew had withdrawn into a shell and become so unlike her usual self. She had aged beyond her years, had no confidence, and could not even speak in the presence of her husband. As the days went by, we got talking and she started confiding in me that she felt trapped in the relationship. She had sacrificed who she was, her needs, dreams, and ambitions to maintain a relationship she thought she needed to be whole. She had started feeling she was not good enough since all her friends had gotten married. So, her only option was to run away from home and be with her husband. Of course, that was just the climax that began with a multitude of other smaller and more innocuous choices that slowly chipped away at her sense of self.

Her final decision was to quit her job as a teacher and become a homemaker and depend on her husband for money to run the house. He was in charge and did not care what she wanted and would not listen to her suggestions or preferences. He claimed he knew what was good for her—after all, he was the man. Her husband left no stone unturned when insulting her or putting her down. He even controlled how she dressed; at his insistence, she wore baggy clothes.

He wanted her well-covered, and to make sure this happened, he bought her all her clothes. He made sure he got her two to three sizes larger than her actual size. She had no friends as he made sure she had broken all ties with even her family members. I asked why she could not stop her husband. She said she loved him a lot and wanted him to be happy; that was why she allowed the change.

And what a total transformation she underwent! She confessed that she was not happy, she was constantly on edge making sure she lived up to his desire. Through prayer and counselling, she received healing. She regained her sense of self-worth and realized she did not need to make herself become someone else to make her husband happy. I introduced her to the Lord and she gradually had a closer walk with God; she developed a personal relationship with God. This boosted her self-esteem; with this newfound confidence, she decided to register for further studies. She is now very happy as God brought healing to her marriage and restored her home and confidence.

You can't control how someone else feels about you. You just need to accept that you can't win them all and that it isn't because you're fatally flawed; it's just how the world works. If you are on the path to winning them all, you will be living a very superficial and suffocating life. Love and prioritize yourself. That is the best way to protect yourself from people who want to hurt you. Love without regret but learn how to say *no* and be as assertive as possible. Do not be bossy, demanding, or clingy, and do not become someone's punching bag because you love them. Remember, love is the easiest and simplest thing to do. You just need to love yourself first before you can love another person or your spouse as you were meant to do. This is because you cannot give what you do not have. Do not overcomplicate things. You need to be happy on your own. Don't depend or base your happiness on her/him. When in a marriage, note that not only love is needed for success, but trust is important and so is honesty. No matter how hard it is to do, trust fully and be honest.

The world is filled with people who are so competitive that all they want to do is be sure they are doing exactly what their neighbours are doing. Their duty is to play catchup and make it look like the idea was theirs all along. Why waste your life on another person's dreams that will never satisfy you? Dream your own dreams and watch them take shape.

You are capable and can do all things through Christ who strengthens you. You have dreams and ambitions and there is nowhere in the Bible that states that as a married person, you cannot fulfill these dreams. Stop limiting yourself and God! Strike forth and be all you want to be!

Be faithful to your own wife and give your love to her alone.

Children that you have by other women will do you no good.

Your children should grow up to help you, not strangers.

So be happy with your wife and find your joy with the woman you married—pretty and graceful as a deer. Let her charms keep you happy; let her surround you with her love.

—Proverbs 5:15–19 (GNTA)

Chapter Seven

Sensuality

Another important aspect of marriage that is often taken for granted is sensuality, which translates into sex for many. However, according to the *Oxford Dictionary,* sensuality is "the enjoyment, expression, or pursuit of physical, especially sexual, pleasure."

Sensuality can make both partners feel great, both emotionally and physically. God made this to bring about intimacy between husband and wife. It has the ability to draw spouses closer to each other. When used appropriately, it strengthens and increases the emotional bonds between a couple and also leads to an increase of goodwill between both spouses. It is not meant to be misused or as bait for your spouse. Sex was created by God for humanity to be used within marriage.

In Genesis 11:27–32, it is made clear that God intended for the first man and wife to build a family through which He would build a nation. Through this nation, God would then bless all the nations of the earth. For this to be possible, sex was necessary so that man and woman could procreate and have a family that God could work with to establish His kingdom.

Another reason for sex was that it was meant for partnership. The word *partnership* means "the state or condition of being a partner; as, to be in partnership with another; to have partnership in the fortunes of a family or a state" *(Webster's Revised Unabridged Dictionary)*. The partnership in question here is that which God made to exist between man and woman. God knew it would not work any other way or perfectly well if the individuals involved did not have equal rights. In Genesis 1:27–28, God created humans (both male and female) in God's own divine image. He made co-rulers; here we had our first king and queen over creation! There was no superiority intended in God's creation of Adam and Eve. We see that God's intent was that of equality of position and authority. He wanted them to rule together! There is a confirmation of this in 1 Corinthians11:3 that states, "But I would have you know that the head of every man is Christ, and the head of the woman is the man and the head of Christ is God." Man and woman were created together and shared the same image of God; they were partners and companions that were to work toward becoming intimately tied together and in one flesh. This intimacy compelled Adam to make the statement "bone of my bones and flesh of my flesh" transcending into the highest form of equality and intimacy. God gave them the pleasure of having full participation in tending the garden and ruling over other creatures. They were not just to do this as they were also mandated in Ephesians 5:21 as follows: "submitting yourselves one to another in the fear of God." We must note here that even though the woman was to obey the husband, please make no mistake in thinking that she was in any way inferior to the man. This only meant that she had to be willing to let the man lead while she supported him.

We see that the two of them, even when naked, were unashamed as they shared each other's company. In this, we also see that Adam's story began with him in loneliness, roaming the garden with just the animals. God, in His infinite wisdom, saw this was not good and brought an end to his solitude as He provided him with companionship in the form of Eve. She was to be a helpmate to Adam, supporting him in the calling God had given him—she was in no way inferior to him.

Sex was also meant for pleasure as seen here in Proverbs 5:15–19:

> Be faithful to your own wife and give
> your love to her alone. Children that
> you have by other women will do you
> no good. Your children should grow
> up to help you, not strangers. So be
> happy with your wife and find your

joy with the woman you married—
pretty and graceful as a deer. Let
her charms keep you happy; let her
surround you with her love.

When I talk about sex being meant for pleasure,
please understand here that I am talking about pleasure
in marriage and not the casual way it is being treated
as if for some experimentation that is done outside
marriage. It must be embraced and appreciated as a
gift from God and not be abused. Our bodies were
meant to give each other pleasure in the marriage not
shared freely among all as it can have very harmful
results. It should be adopted in marriage to build your
relationship with your spouse and be something both
of you can savour. From this you can see that only
when you are married should you be involved in a
sexual relationship with your spouse. When practiced
in marriage, it can reduce the greatest of tensions.
When couples selflessly give of their bodies and offer
themselves to each other, they renew marital affection
and create intimacy. Sex can bind two hearts together
and pave the way for greater understanding and love.
It possesses the power to diffuse all built-up tensions
and nullify most underlying displeasure, problems,
and dissatisfaction that might have cropped up or have
lain unresolved between the partners.

I have often heard people say they have no interest
in sex because their spouses are not good or are not
fulfilling their sexual needs and they have come up

with several reasons why this is so. I would like to use this opportunity to say that sexual intimacy does not happen overnight. Just like anything that involves marriage, it needs effort and hard work. It must be nurtured, kindled, built, and rebuilt continuously. You must keep the fire burning! This is because couples are on their journey of discovery and need to work toward intimacy. Also, couples are exposed to a lot of stress and pressure in their daily routine, so they might be tired and stressed and not want to explore any form of intimacy at the end of a busy day. Talk to each other and find a way of resolving the issues that plague you.

Sex was also meant for protection, according to Proverbs 5:20 and 1 Corinthians 6:12–26, 7:2–5: "Place your sexuality under the Lordship of our savior Jesus Christ to maintain its purity and divine purpose and you would not have so many problems." Hebrews 13:4 enjoins that we should "Let marriage be held in honour among all, and let the marriage bed be undefiled." This means that you should let the marriage bed be without sin; do not sin in your sexual relations. Now, we have seen that sin is whatever is not from faith and goes against the precepts of God. Sin is what you feel and think and do when you are not taking God at his word and resting in his promises. In your bid to fulfill your sexual intimacy, you must be careful that you keep your sexual relations free from any act or attitude that does not conform to the Word of God. Your character must be devoid of anything sinful and must emerge out of the contentment that comes from the confidence you have in God's promises.

Paul says in Ephesians 6:16–17:

> In addition to all this, take up the shield of faith, with which you can extinguish all the flaming arrows of the evil one. Take the helmet of salvation and the sword of the Spirit, which is the word of God. And pray in the Spirit on all occasions with all kinds of prayers and requests.

As couples, we must not rely on our own power to fight the devil but ward him off with prayer through the Spirit of God. I remember some years ago, a senior member of our women's fellowship came to see me as she had had a fight with her husband. Her resolution before she came to see me was to deny him sex to bring him back in line. I found this intriguing and asked how often she did this and if it worked for her; her response was that she did so whenever he misbehaved with her for some extended period, after which he would come begging. I must confess she sounded very smug and happy about this as she reckoned she had valid reasons for withholding sexual intimacy from her husband. Unbeknownst to her, she was walking in sin, not in obedience, as this action is not in any way Christ-like. She had chosen the wrong path and was at risk of inviting sin into her marriage. In some marriages, withholding of sex exposes a spouse to great sins like pornography, prostitution, adultery, and many more. You must consciously remind yourself of the fact that Paul in 1 Corinthians 7:2–5 states:

> But since sexual immorality is occurring, each man should have sexual relations with his own wife, and each woman with her own husband. The husband should fulfill his marital duty to his wife, and likewise the wife to her husband. The wife does not have authority over her own body but yields it to her husband. In the same way, the husband does not have authority over his own body but yields it to his wife. Do not deprive each other except perhaps by mutual consent and for a time, so that you may devote yourselves to prayer. Then come together again so that Satan will not tempt you because of your lack of self-control.

If married men and women do not remain physically intimate with each other regularly, they are setting themselves up for sin. If they withhold sex from each other, they are setting up their spouse for sin—the Bible enjoins all married couples not to abstain from sexual relations for too long so that they do not allow the devil to gain a foothold in their home. Sexual relations, as I mentioned earlier, are a gift from God and should be used as a means of grace as this is an avenue for overcoming the temptation to sin. The Bible further states in 1 Corinthians 7:3–5 that "in the process of the two becoming one flesh, their bodies are at each other's disposal." They now have rights over each other's bodies. Each has the right to lay claim to the other's body for sexual satisfaction and pleasure.

Most of us as couples are limited in our sensual experience because of the self-doubt that plagues us. A careful look at your bodies will reveal to you that God meant you to enjoy and revel in each other, to appreciate and enjoy the differences in your bodies, just like Adam and Eve did before the fall. However, realize that because we live in an imperfect world, even the beauty queens have insecurities that make them feel uncomfortable exposing some of their body parts. Adam and Eve were naked in the garden of Eden and had no yardstick by which to compare themselves. There were no manmade standards to hold on to that would dictate how perfect they were or were not. After all, there were no people to judge nor compare themselves to as this was not the focal point. They were just ecstatic that they had each other! Adam and Eve enjoyed each other's company and focused on the journey of discovery. With no distractions, they developed an understanding of one another and were focused on the inward beauty, not the imperfections in each other's bodies. Although they were not by any standard perfect, nowhere is it recorded that they felt uncomfortable appreciating or revelling in their bodies. There were self-imposed limitations, manmade shields, or boundaries between them as they ran around and tended the garden in all their naked glory. They also did not lack anything, nor felt the need for the courage to face each other in their vulnerability and nakedness as they were innocent and unashamed. They just appreciated and revelled in each other!

Due to the media, television, and books, depicting man's ideas of the perfect figure, height, weight, and so on, you develop insecurities as you perceive that you fall short of these ideals. Because of this, you do not feel sexy or good enough for your spouse. You become very uncomfortable at your spouse's mere mention of intimacy. You start putting up barriers, which lead to frustration, breakdown in communication and separation.

I once had a client who sought my help because she felt she was ugly and unappealing. As we got talking, I went through a series of questions to determine what approach to use and she said, "That is me" so fast before I could finish what I was about to say whenever the topic centred on her body or physical appearance. At the end of our session, she said, "Can I be sincere with you? I know I am really ugly, and I would need all the help I can get to be a little okay." This brought tears to my eyes which I quickly wiped away. I could see she lacked a lot of confidence in herself as it was so difficult to make her believe or start feeling that she was not ugly at all.

On further queries, I realized that she became like that due to the several years of abuse at her husband's hands. He found it a great sport to compare her to the beautiful figures splashed on magazine covers and televisions. She could not remember a time when her husband did not communicate that he felt repulsed by her appearance! This destroyed her self-confidence and rendered her insecure. The rare moments of intimacy she had with her husband had been very rushed and clumsy. Sometimes these took place only when her husband was drunk! She always dreaded these occasions as she felt little or no connection with him. She felt obliged to perform her duty and wanted it to end.

This is entirely the opposite of what God said or intended when He created man and woman, as seen in Genesis 1:27: "So God created man in his own image, in the image of God he created him; male and female he created them." If you are created in God's image, why should you not be able to appreciate how wonderfully you have been made? Why should you allow another person to dictate how you should be and act?

God's desire for couples is to experience great, satisfying, and enduring pleasure in one another! He does not want barriers that would make you feel constrained or limited in your enjoyment. His desire is that you should be fulfilled, and your enjoyment should be heightened, not dampened. This is one aspect wherein as couples, you have been granted the freedom to experiment and communicate with each other about everything, especially sex and sensuality! God does not want you to be timid with each other but wants you to exercise the liberty He has granted you for your mutual pleasure in the bedroom.

I was listening to a wonderful Christian woman many years ago counselling her daughter on sexual relations and intimacy with her husband. What caught my attention was that she asked a rhetorical question in a very condescending manner and it went like this: "I wonder what they see in sexual intercourse or relationships? I just cannot get my head around this!" On introspection and further reflection, I realized that she had been brought up to believe that any interest in one's sexuality/sensuality was dirty and considered a sin. This is not surprising because many Christian couples have no idea what freedom they have in the bedroom with their spouses. God has made it so easy for you to enjoy each other! Instead of fantasizing about sex, talk to your spouse, and enjoy God's gift. You are married and it is not a sin to be sensual with your spouse.

This is the time to remove all self-imposed restrictions and inhibitions on yourselves that have nothing to do with God's perspective. God made the marriage institution a safe place for a husband and wife to explore, experiment, laugh, and get lost in sensational pleasure. Be free with each other because God is not poised with a sledgehammer waiting to strike you down. The reverse is the case because He is pleased when you revel in each other and enjoy his gift to you. Have you ever given someone a gift and he never put it to use because he did not like it? How did that make you feel? God wants you to use the gift of sensuality to enhance your marital bond with your spouse. He does not want you to go and engage in an extramarital affair to be able to experience the sexual satisfaction He has granted you. If anything, He cautions against this.

There is nothing spiritual or moral about limiting sexual pleasure in marriage. God is the greatest advocate for your pleasure—not the pleasure that is sweet for a season, but the deep, profound satisfaction that only grows sweeter with time. God wants you to reserve sex, sexual fantasies, and sexual expression only for your husband or wife. It means more than just what you do physically, but what fascinates you, what you look at, and what you think about. To reinforce this, let us take another look at 1 Corinthians 7:3–4:

> The husband should fulfill his marital
> duty to his wife, and likewise the wife
> to her husband. The wife does not
> have authority over her own body
> but yields it to the husband. In the

> same way, the husband does not have
> authority over his body but yields to
> his wife.

This is as self-explanatory as possible and cannot be underestimated. Adultery is not only when you have an affair with anyone apart from your spouse; it includes fantasy, pornography, online relationships, erotica, and the list goes on. This seems like a pretty strict standard.

Jesus goes on to advise us on how to deal with temptation. He said in Matthew 5:29, "If your right eye causes you to sin, gouge it out and throw it away. It is better for you to lose one part of your body than for your whole body to be thrown into hell." This message could not have been made any clearer. Jesus wants you to get rid of whatever causes you to sin in your heart! If it is an avenue for temptation, get rid of the books, the TV, or whatever medium grants or provides access for you to sin! Cut off the ties that are luring and tempting you to sin. I am sure God, in His omniscient ability, knew that the feelings of pleasure, anticipation, gratitude, and release husbands or wives get from indulging in such experiences can make them less satisfied with the affection they get from their spouses. This results in feelings of frustration and resentment. This warning is not to be taken lightly, as Christ was serious about it.

Sin and God cannot dance or be even aligned together as the Bible says in 2 Corinthians 6:14: "Do not be yoked together with unbelievers. For what do righteousness and wickedness have in common? Or what fellowship can light have with darkness?" Throw out the porn. Stop flirting with anything that causes you to think, lust, or fantasize about someone other than your spouse. It is not only when you engage in sex with someone other than your wife that you have committed adultery. Your thoughts, eyes, and ears can lead you to sin too. God has made your spouse and endowed her/him with all attributes to provide you with sexual satisfaction. You don't need a Mr. or Ms. Universe because your spouse already is one!

If, for a moment, you thought this was nothing, permit me to take your imagination somewhere: Think about what it's like when you meet your husband or wife's emotional and sexual needs? Everything about them is different as there is an air of anticipation and satisfaction around them. They are excited and can hardly wait to lay their eyes on you! In fact, it is a herculean task to keep your thoughts from the wonder you have experienced! You find yourself smiling secretly as you remember what has transpired between you. This is because of the way you had made him/her feel. The beauty of this is that you do not need to be rich or a millionaire to make each other feel this way! You just need to use your God-given attributes. Imagine the power you both have! If you believe in your relationship and are committed to one another, you can make your marriage a huge success.

After all, sex is a lot more than just sharing your body—it is a journey of a lifetime of intimacy. Do not expect to have fulfillment when you disrespect one another! It would be very difficult as the hurt lingers on and is sometimes difficult to put away without complete resolution or forgiveness. So, forgive one another as lovemaking means surrendering yourself to the one you love! Figuring out boundaries together gives you great opportunities to seek the Lord's wisdom, and to learn how to love each other more deeply and in very special ways.

Wives, always bear in mind that your husbands are wired differently from you. Have you ever taken a moment to examine your husband's behaviour after lovemaking? Have you not realized that there is something that seems a little different about him? Does it not occur to you that your husband seems to treat you differently after lovemaking? He's more attentive, more affectionate, and more appreciative. Let us flip the coin for a minute here to the ladies. Husbands, have you ever taken the time to examine the change in your wife after satisfying lovemaking? She has a glow about her and would do anything to please you because she feels powerful, beautiful, and, above all, loved!

This is not a mind game! The change is because she is made that way—to bond with you after intimacy. Do you remember? As I mentioned above, some deposits have taken place! He feels emotionally closer to you and safer with you. Why should he not?

Your husband depends on you not only to be present in sickness and joy but to be his unwavering partner in his battle against sexual temptation, and you have just helped him win big time! You have just convinced him that you are solidly with him and that you are a key component in his victory. You have left no stone unturned; you went all the way and helped in destroying the enemies' plan against your marriage. You are the only woman in the world whom he can look at, touch sensually, allow himself to be weak and vulnerable with, without compromising his integrity! He would not feel like a thief! You are a vital part of him, and your hurt is his and vice versa.

You are finally connected to him in a very different way as you have embraced and recognized the one aspect of his life that dominates him physically, spiritually, emotionally, and relationally! So, make a conscious effort not to ignore or minimize this aspect and always remember that it is a gift, a blessing from God. "The blessing of the LORD makes rich, and he adds no sorrow with it" (Proverbs 10:22). Remove these newfound ideas of marriage being some form of torture or a life sentence. These are lies peddled by those who do not want to commit in the real sense. Understand that God made it so you can be fulfilled as spouses through it. He makes no mistakes.

In Hebrews 13:4, Paul enjoins, "Marriage should be honored by all, and the marriage bed kept pure, for God will judge the adulterer and all the sexually immoral." We see here that loyalty to one's spouse is not only mandatory but a prerequisite for a successful marriage. I hear people explaining away their reasons for infidelity with statements like "She was not the one I had in mind to marry, or my parents forced me into marrying her/him."

Well, it's time to wake up and smell the roses! What is of utmost importance is the fact that you are married now to the person and you owe it to them to be the best you can be. If you were so against her as a wife, you could from the very beginning have spared each other the heartache by refusing or opting out of the marriage! When you exchanged those vows, you made promises to her and those promises are very important to her and they hold true. She is ready to fulfill her part of the promise, but it is your responsibility to be true to both of you and meet her halfway. It is not a union that is formed based on our whims and caprices. It is meant to last for life. So, what better time than now for you to start working on it?

As soon as the vows are made or taken, your life, destinies, even your blessings become intertwined. You are no longer separate entities but one. With the promise and vows made, you have boldly relinquished a hold on the "me" and made it "us/we." You have become soulmates, and if any harm comes to one, the other person feels the pain and suffers too. From now onward, you will be rewarded for each other's deeds. Thinking you can do whatever pleases you does not come into the question here because whatever hurts or worries the other person automatically worries you. You complement each other, and like my elders would like to say often, you do not look good without each other. You are not each other's keepers, but you are your spouse, husband or wife.

The big question then is, why don't we exercise this God-given power? If it is a great gift from God, then when you are angry with your spouse or if you want to manipulate him, is it wrong or right to use sex as a tool? You are creating an avenue for discord to be sewn into your marriage; instead, communicate your feelings in a calm, positive, and productive way. The Bible advises that we should not withhold sex except by mutual consent in some instances/cases where you are fasting (1 Corinthians 7:5). If not, it can then become very destructive and consume everything in its bid for fulfillment. What began as an innocent and playful experiment could soon escalate out of control and become a burning inferno.

A sexual sin that comprises adultery is stealing also. Everybody loses when adultery raises its ugly head. Proverbs 6:32–33 says, "But a man who commits adultery has no sense; whoever does so destroys himself. Blows and disgrace are his lot and his shame will never be wiped away." Nothing remains the same once adultery is allowed into the marriage. Situations that were once enjoyable now pale in comparison with what is happening outside. We must remain true and faithful to our vows by disciplining our hands, eyes, ears, and heart.

Now, this is it! All of us claim to be very disciplined, but how many of us can really attest to the fact that we can control our eyes? Spouses who think they can just play the field without getting burnt—after all, they have everything under control—have another thing coming. Well, this is very dangerous because a foundation of betrayal has been laid, and it takes divine intervention and forgiveness from your spouse to rebuild the broken promise and reestablish trust. Eliminate all distractions and temptations that might cause you to stray. A good thing to do is to limit the time you spend on interacting on social media and other compromising situations Place a higher value on the time you spend with your spouse. Always think about stimulating ways you can improve your marriage and incorporate fun things both of you can do together that would not only ease your spouse's burdens but draw you closer to one another.

Let your conduct be without covetousness and be content with such things as you have. For He Himself has said: "I will never leave you nor forsake you."

—Hebrews 13:5

Chapter Eight

Commitment and Balance

For a marriage to be successful, there is a need for both individuals to achieve balance and determine to be committed to the relationship. This is where there is parity between the spouses. A marriage where one partner feels that he is the more deserving of the two always leaves a sour taste in the mouth of the other partner. Some cases arise where the other individual decides to remain quiet so that peace might reign in the home. This in no way shows that the marriage is a happy one. Rather, both partners are just going through the motions. For all aspects of marriage to work, there must be a balance. The husband must not think he rules the roost because he is the breadwinner. You cannot, in all truthfulness, love a self-centred, and selfish man or woman who feels you are just a little higher than the maidservant! Or that you are just there to perform some duties he would not have been able to in your absence. Be aware that your spouse knows when she is being relegated to the background.

An emotional and lifelong commitment to a marriage is a very conscious choice or decision couples must make. Therefore emotional, physical and psychological commitment would mean that you are willing to give up your freedom and choices that would seek to become hindrances in your home to become each other's strength, shoulder each other's responsibility, work in sync with each other, and in so doing, learn to love, forgive, and respect one another. I am not trying to say that as spouses, you need to lose your individuality and become just a shadow of yourself. What I mean here is that you purposefully commit to being the best you can be for yourself and your spouse. Do not be afraid to say your spouse loves you, and be bold enough to say she/he made a mistake and needs forgiveness. If you want your marriage to last, you both must commit to doing whatever it takes to make the marriage work, and that means accepting and knowing that there are going to be many times when you are just not going to get your way. It is necessary to understand that it is not only about you, and you are going to have to be okay with putting your needs away for a moment so someone else can thrive.

Marriage is about both of you. No one has been assigned as the maid or the master in this relationship. You must commit to helping one another in the house and making a success of it. What I mean by "commit" is that you both put in 100 percent of your time, effort, energy, dedication, and above all, love into this relationship to make it last. Stop expecting each other or the one conceived of as the lesser of you to continue sacrificing and giving up herself or himself until she or he is lost and unrecognizable.

Throw away all options at your disposal but that of success at making each other the best and most important person in your home and outside the home. You must become each other's priority. Work together to foster love and unity.

Marriage is not a testing arena. Once you get into it, know that you belong to the same team. Commit to fighting together as a team against everything that seeks to destroy your marriage and continue working on your relationship for you will be with each other for a long time. Marriage is for life. Committed love is one of the keys to a happy marriage. It means you have decided and chosen to be absolutely committed to your spouse. You would not continue having relationships or dates with other men or women. In doing this, you understand that there is going to be no room for cheating or philandering. It does not just happen overnight but takes some time and demands that you be vulnerable to each other. This committed love is an opportunity to share your feelings, listen to one another and support one another through all the adversities that would come your way. It takes a lot of emotionally committed love to get through the ups and downs and tough times that you will encounter in your lives. But before you can have more, do you know what it really means?

As defined by the *Cambridge Dictionary,* the word "commitment" is the willingness to give your time and energy to something that you believe in [marriage], or a promise or firm decision to do something [for your spouse]. (Note: I added the words in brackets.) Committed love can be divided into three areas when talking about or referring to marriage. In lifelong commitment, the couple (husband and wife) must personally determine or resolve that they both will fulfill the responsibilities and obligations of their marriage and home. This is because for intimacy to begin in your marriage, there must be a real emotional commitment, the determination that no matter the odds or difficulties you encounter, your priority would be the welfare of your marriage.

Getting married and saying "I do" is the easiest thing to do. However, problems arise when you suddenly discover that you know absolutely nothing about marriage. You are hit with the sudden realization that marriage is not what you wanted. Because some of you, even after tying the knot, are still not committed and have not decided to give up other options and invest your all into the relationship. Your exit mentality is still in place and you are basically waiting for the tide to change. Little wonder then, that, most of you just go through the motions without ever reaching your greatest potential in attending intimacy and closeness because you have never psychologically committed to being in that relationship or working at it to reach the stage where you can begin to enjoy the security essential for true intimacy.

With the advent and rise of live-in relationships, the word *commitment* has lost its flare. People cohabit for a length of time and become partners. That does not mean they are committed to one another. I hear people saying, "Jack and I don't feel that we need a piece of paper to make us happy." Others have said, "Who needs to be married when I can just move out when I don't want the relationship anymore?" As far-fetched as this might sound, it is true. Some parents are so proud to kick their girls out of the home to live with their boyfriends! One told me she was finally free because her sixteen-year-old had moved in with her boyfriend! What a life! As sad as it sounds, this is the real truth. The question here is, what future do you envision for your little girl? Have you equipped her adequately with the necessary tools to move out at that age? Do you really want her to live happily ever after? Did you even teach her anything about marriage? What expectations do you have concerning her life? Yet we wonder why divorce is at its peak now. I had a "friend" who was in a common-law marriage for twenty years and within this period, she had moved out more than three times to live with other guys. The reason? She had fallen in love with them only to go back to the first guy! Dare I ask here if love is a light switch, we can turn on and off?

What are we teaching our younger generations? Do not forget that your actions are your children's greatest teachers or coaches. We are all role models to someone whether we like it or not we do not need to be celebrities to be this. We have the ability to influence someone somewhere even if it is not our immediate family members. Where are the values our parents instilled in us? If a man loves you, he will do anything to get a ring on your finger! So why settle for less? Do not throw yourself at some man just in the name of partnership or marriage! Remember you are precious, beautiful, and wonderfully made! Can I just chip in here that the greatest relationship you can have is with yourself! You must learn to love and accept yourself unconditionally. Be authentic and like yourself just the way you are and never stop working towards being the best possible you. Accept yourself for who you are for only then can you do justice to any relationship you decide to enter into. You deserve better! Even if your parents do not want you in their home again, get a job, rent an apartment and carry on with your life. Under no circumstances should you settle for less. Wait for the right guy God has designed for you to turn up. Never settle for frogs; the fairy-tale era is gone! You do not need to go kissing ten frogs to see which one becomes your prince!

You are more than enough! Note that wrong choices produce long-lasting problems. This can be seen in Genesis 16:5, 21:8–21, 25:6 between Abraham and Sarah, Hagar and Sarah, where Sarah was too impatient to wait for the Lord's promise to come to pass and went ahead to try and speed the promise of a child into being by giving her maidservant to her husband to bear the covenant child. That led to so many problems in their lives and even in the world! This must sound very familiar because most of us like quick fixes and are so impatient that, even if the message were delivered to us by the Lord Himself, we would still not be ready for it to come to pass. We decide we need it and it must be according to our own timing, not later, and are guilty of second-guessing the Lord and trying to do things our way as it is always said, "God helps those who help themselves!" The mindset here is, why not try fixing it and let us see how it goes? Your way might even be better! Attention, please! I have gone through the Bible so many times and I have been unable to find this commandment or teaching. Whatever happened to "Be still, and know that I am God; I will be exalted among the nations, I will be exalted in the earth" (Psalm 46:10)? God is never rushed; He does everything at the right time. He who formed the earth and all creation in six days and rested on the seventh knows how important timing is, and He would just answer at the perfect time. We must just believe!

Know that no one can open their heart to a man or woman who is not emotionally, psychologically committed nor trustworthy as they fear they might be deserted or forsaken. When the vows are taken and we promise till death do us part, it is a promise that we are in the marriage to stay. It is entirely voluntary, and you do not need to feel forced, intimidated, blackmailed, or coerced into doing anything. This aspect of commitment is more than mere words; it is a promise to keep going, no matter what the circumstances. This creates long-standing trust that leads to intimacy and bliss in the marriage and home. Never make each other feel as if you are running this race alone. Emotional and lifelong commitment is a promise to stay together no matter the trials as you know both of you would weather any storm that comes your way. As mentioned before, it does not happen overnight. Be ready to be honest, truthful and also trust each other. Some of you threaten divorce when you encounter problems.

I have often heard some clients say that they are tired and cannot do it anymore! Some also say that they regret getting married! My first impulse is to respond that this is not the way to go here. Then I am forced to pause and wonder at this. What was their intention in getting married? Did they seek God's will for their marriage? God the creator made marriage and wanted it to be fulfilling for both partners. Why do people have this reaction then? You were made to be helpers for each other, not Lord/master and servant. If this was your thinking, then you have got another thing coming. This is because you are not doing it the way God intended. Seek His face and let Him show you what His desire is for your marriage

The Bible in Isaiah 53:6 says, "We all, like sheep, have gone astray, each of us has turned to our own way; and the LORD has laid on him the iniquity of us all." Yes, we have all failed! No one cares about what God intended marriages to be like nor what He wants us to do; we all do what we feel like and end up ruining everything. You just want to get married, so you do so with all the wrong ideas. Some people say they feel lonely, so they get married just to fill their need for companionship. Others get married because they think it is just the right time; they do what everyone does—just get married. When will this penchant to do what everyone else is doing come to an end? When do you really look at yourself and do what you need to do, to make yourself not like your neighbour but position yourself in a way that the Lord will begin to use you as He has planned?

In this male-dominated world, where men feel they can never go wrong, some women might feel they must give up something for the men to show their commitment. In some relationships, this means that the woman will give up a lot for the man before he does the same for her or even starts thinking in terms of making a commitment. What do you expect? After years of sacrifice, you wake up and suddenly realize you have been doing all the giving! Will being shocked be justified? Being astounded and disillusioned to find that he is not ready and will not commit is just an understatement! The next available option is to get out as soon as possible. If not, you decide to compromise your self-respect and just bear all the atrocities dished out to you.

Another pertinent point worthy of note is that some of you who refuse to face issues and work through them (especially some of the men) are not in any way contributing to the well-being of your marriage. You would rather sweep the issues under the carpet or behave as if nothing really matters! A very common cop-out is to walk away from any confrontation that makes you feel uncomfortable. Sorry to burst your bubble! The issue is not resolved until it is dealt with in the right way: "communication," the absence of which will result in a lack of trust and intimacy and a breakdown in the relationship. Excuse me! This is not grade school! Neither are you in a science laboratory conducting an experiment to see how far you can go! Man up and do the right thing: Learn to talk to each other and resolve issues. Your silence could be interpreted to mean you could not care less or, put directly, you do not care about what the other person or your spouse does. The marriage could fail for all you care! This attitude is not only condescending, but you are taking your spouse for granted! Speak up! Be the man or woman God created you to be.

It must always be remembered that marriage is the union of two people, and your commitment to one another is the glue that binds it. Your silence is not in any way going to help this relationship become stronger. Rather, it will set you back and make you strangers. God's intention for marriage was to create a relationship where both spouses would be each other's companion. When you have hobbies and friends who have ultimately taken the place of your God-given spouses, how do you expect to meet each other's needs for companionship and build a relationship? Some of you hardly talk! Talking to each other about issues results in a happy union because you understand one another. There are no second-guessing or unresolved issues between you. It is your responsibility to make sure that intimacy in your marriage is not compromised nor damaged in any way. Work toward increasing communion between you and your partner. The Bible states in Hebrews 13:5 that we must "Let our conduct be without covetousness and be content with such things as you have. For He Himself has said: 'I will never leave you nor forsake you.'" Get your priorities right if you want your marriage to be a success. Do what is best for both of you, not what you want as an individual. You are a team! So, roll up your sleeves and get to work!

This brings me to the second aspect of commitment, which is commonly referred to as "moral commitment." It is a known fact that morality has a big role to play in marriage. The moral aspect is what enables you to make the right choices concerning you, your spouse, your family, and your marriage.

When the word *moral* is mentioned, we are immediately brought to a startling halt! Do people still talk about morality? Is it not too staid or ancient? What does that word, *moral*, really mean? Does it apply to everybody, or is it just a few people belonging to a certain class that need to possess this attribute? Regardless of the questions asked, the answer remains the same: Well, everybody needs to have morality, not only for a successful marriage but for successful living and for success in other relationships. We live in a society where little or no attention is paid to our conduct; we live to please our selfish selves. This can be seen even in the way we handle our professional obligations and personal lives. It has become very difficult to differentiate between right and wrong. This attitude has spilled over into marriage with spouses living to please themselves, paying no attention to what the other person feels or wants.

Your internal values are very important in this aspect of commitment, especially when you talk about marriage. Your personal beliefs, who you are, what you think, your orientation—all matter in the relationship. In marriage, when you are morally committed to your spouse, it is the case that both of you are acutely aware of the sense of right or wrong that is the guiding force in decision-making. Spouses bound by this will be careful not to hurt each other nor will they delve into casual relationships nor commit adultery when they feel the urge to do so. Being morally committed involves doing good and avoiding evil, condemning promiscuous behaviour, and putting your spouse first in all aspects. Doing this is not one person's responsibility but a joint effort from both partners.

A spouse who has a high level of moral commitment knows the right thing to do for a blissful marriage. They know they belong to one another, so they are both committed to keeping their bodies and souls connected and focused on each other. They will not cheat on each other nor will they betray each other's trust. They honour their marriage and the promises they have made to each other. We must look at the promise our Lord God made to us! He said, "He will never leave nor forsake us." He is committed to us at the utmost and highest level with no regard nor intention of breaking His relationship with us. He has promised, and this means that He will never physically leave nor turn His heart away from us nor forsake us. His word is true and sure. He is physically and emotionally committed to staying with us! He wants the best for us. So, in marriage, we must be physically and emotionally committed to staying with each other and making it work.

Remember, we are made in God's image, and we are to hold our marriage and spouse in the highest esteem. We must have deaf ears to what society dictates as individual rights, personal freedom, and principles, but determine only to do what is right for our marriage. Remember, that satan would try all his tricks to derail you from your God-ordained ministries and calling. The devil's agents have invented many distractions to destroy the institution of marriage. The devil will be happiest if the marriage institution dissolves. Determine to give your marriage its pride of place and put your spouse's needs above your own. Now is the time to throw far away that pleasure-seeking idea you have been nursing if you have not already done so. This is because when you focus only on your needs and forget about your partner's needs, disappointment, irritation, discontentment, and apathy set in.

This will not end here as you now start imagining how good your life would have been if you had been unmarried or with another partner. You are doing yourself a disservice; whenever you compare yourself to another person, the stakes just keep getting higher and higher. You never feel fulfilled or happy as there is no killer as slow and lethal as *comparison*. It gradually saps away your happiness and joy, leaving you empty and bitter, always needing more as you keep looking at what others have. You will even begin to feel that your happiness is dependent on what others can bring into your life. Sometimes we have everything in a relationship but fail to realize each other's value as we keep comparing ourselves or competing with others. The question here is when do you stop, take a long look at yourself, and be real? Ask yourself if you are really satisfied in your relationship! Trust me, stop the comparison and you will see that the reverse is always the case when you focus on you and your spouse's needs. There is great pleasure derived from doing little things that bring joy to the heart. Love and intimacy increase when you help each other or engage in doing things such as little as chores together and looking out for one another.

A form of commitment that always gets overlooked is structural commitment. I would not blame you if you were to ask what structure has to do with marriage or commitment. For anything worthwhile to be built or to happen, there is a need for structure. The Bible says in Psalm 127:1 "Unless the LORD builds the house, the builders labor in vain. Unless the LORD watches over the city, the guards stand watch in vain." If the foundation of your marriage is not based on the right source, the Lord, all your efforts will be in vain. Try a little reality check here: How can you buy equipment you know nothing about and totally ignore the instructions that came with it? How do you go into marriage without the Lord of the marriage to guide and order your steps?

In marriage, structural commitment refers to the pledge made between spouses to stay in the relationship despite the levels of personal and moral commitments. Do you remember the vows you took? The promises you made to each other? You might have pledged that you would be married till death do you part or something along those lines! On what did you base or build your marriage? The only provision for dissolution of marriage is death as seen in the Bible in Romans 7:2–3, which states:

> By law a married woman is bound
> to her husband as long as he is alive,
> but if her husband dies, she is released
> from the law that binds her to him. So
> then, if she has sexual relations with
> another man while her husband is still
> alive, she is called an adulteress. But if
> her husband dies, she is released from
> that law and is not an adulteress if she
> marries another man.

This applies to both spouses, not just the woman. Are you willing to work hard to make sure that your union is successful? That it is based on the precepts of the Bible?

Most people opt for marriage just with the concept of structural commitment in mind. They want to have a comfortable life, so they look for someone they think will be able to fit the bill and provide them with all the luxury they crave. At this juncture, there is no consideration for the outcome of such a union. They are satisfied so long as the person fulfills their need for external factors such as finances, social relationships, and societal expectations. This, on its own, cannot make a marriage work. Your commitment must be solid so that these factors and many others cannot become threats to your marriage. Bear in mind that great marriages do not just happen but are based on a deep commitment that sets aside all options but one—*to stay and make it work!* Consciously avoid all things that would have adverse effects on your marriage if its structure is weak. Instead of spending your time with friends who know it all and are envious of your relationship, spend time with your spouse. Remember that those you usually keep company with contribute toward moulding your character.

A wise man was often heard saying, "Show me your friends and I will tell you who you are." You are like your friends no matter how vehemently you try to deny this. The usual crowd you keep company with moulds and influences you. If you spend time with a promiscuous group of friends, it is only a matter of time before you fall prey to the herd mentality, break your marital vows, promises, and become like them! Sometimes it is not only the promises that are broken, but you change so much that a look in the mirror will reveal a very different you! Be cognizant of the fact that it is not only the person that changes altogether. The things or ideals you once held dear become so useless, lame, and unimportant to you that you begin to wonder at their validity.

You settle and become just like your friends. Sometimes you become even more paltry than those friends and ultimately become even worse than those whom you had abhorred or hung out with. The Bible warns in 1 Corinthians 15:33–34 that we should not be misled: "Bad company corrupts good character. Come back to your senses as you ought and stop sinning; for there are some who are ignorant of God—I say this to your shame." In other words, when we associate with or take delight in the company of people with worldly morals, we run the risk of mimicking their behaviour, their language, and their habits. Before long, we are no longer of Christ but of the world, with its denial of God as the absolute authority, its rejection of the Bible as the Word of God, and its ideology of relative morality. Then you start forsaking the assembly of the brethren.

It does not end here, as it is not only the people that influence you but the places you are fond of going to. If you hang out in shady places, those places become a part of you that is so important and inadvertently, you are soon swamped with temptations. Could we take a moment here and ask ourselves this question: When do you spend time with your spouse doing enjoyable activities and building your family together? Some of you act as if you are married to the places you visit! It is like there is a roll call you have to answer to. You make it a point to go there immediately after leaving your office and the sorry excuse is that you had a hard day at work! Surely you deserved to go somewhere and unwind! Hello! I suggest you seek professional help as this has gone beyond the point of relaxation; you are suffering from a greater problem.

> Do not be deceived: God cannot be mocked. A man reaps what he sows. Whoever sows to please their flesh, from the flesh will reap destruction; whoever sows to please the Spirit,

from the Spirit will reap eternal life.
(Galatians 6:7–8).

Well, what a pity that you feel that the shady places you hang out at are better than the home you are supposed to help build! Men, can you imagine what state you would be in if your wife decided to go hang out somewhere after work every day? Do you think being a woman, she has no wish to unwind? Trust me, your spouse's needs are just the same as yours! You get what you give! Why do you dishonour your marriage? Why are you letting selfishness crop into your homes? Where is it written that it is the man's sole responsibility or privilege to unwind? The funniest thing is that the guilty party always feels justified in this act. You do not remember that the more you do this, the sooner you usher in the herd mentality; it takes over and out goes any commitment or desire to be in the relationship. You are to build a very healthy and vital relationship with your spouse! How will this be possible if you are never home on time? The next thing that will crop up is that you feel you cannot live together or stay married. Who caused this problem? It did not come about as a result of incompatibility as most of you are very fast to make this excuse. The blame is on your failure to do what God wanted you to do from the very beginning when He created a helpmeet for you. He wanted you to have a relationship, companionship with your spouse so you will not be lonely and find yourself bored out of your wit's end! The first thing to do here is to go back to the basics and develop a very warm, caring, loving, and thriving companionship with your spouse.

The devil is the deceiver and accuser of the brethren! He comes to steal, to kill, and to destroy! He does not need much prompting to come into your homes and marriages and destroy them! He will destroy everything you hold dear! Your behaviour and failure to build love and companionship with one another have just left a door wide open for him and he needs no second bidding. He is always punctual when offered an invitation, but very slow to leave as he makes sure when he leaves, he has destroyed everything! Do you want to take this chance and give him the opportunity? How important is your marriage to you?

Marriage is a relationship based on a commitment that delivers or offers true and lasting intimacy and satisfaction for both spouses. This can't happen if both spouses do not have a relationship with the Lord. It is common knowledge that difficulties take the glow out of marriage—you must be ready to reexamine your priorities and do some deep heart/ soul searching. I have heard a lot of people say that they never bargained for what they got! They thought it was just going to be all roses! My response is always "Well, you did not take a good look at the roses; they do have thorns that hurt when you do not handle them with care!" So is marriage if not handled carefully and worked on relentlessly. Sadly, we have a culture of doing things just because! Don't just go with the flow, determine to be the difference and lead by example! Decide to commit emotionally, psychologically and lifelong. Before you can really commit, make sure you have a relationship with Jesus as this is the only way you will be able to face all the challenges you are exposed to. Seek Him and be confident in the decisions and choices you have made and stick to them. Determine to be that couple whose marriage does not end in divorce! The statistics projected are also a distraction, so that you do not work hard and try keeping your marriage strong. Treasure each other and work on your marriage. Fight and keep the devil out of your lives.

Both of you must make conscious choices each day for yourselves, marriage, and family. How important to you is the vow you made to each other in front of God and witnesses? To live together until one of you dies, no matter what might happen? To share your sorrows and joys, poverty, and plenty, sickness and health? Is the emotional, psychological and lifelong commitment still of the same importance to you? Remember this, no matter what you might decide, commitment is a very conscious choice. Throw away all options at your disposal but that of success. Be very conscious of what you do with your time. Take stock of where you spend your time. What activity takes the bulk of your time? There are not matters to be treated with levity! Some of you spend more time in bars and other shady places than you do in your homes! Stop neglecting one another!

The worst part is I am not talking about unbelieving husbands and wives but acclaimed Christians and believers! This can make or break a commitment. No matter how much your spouse complains, you turn a deaf ear! After all, he/she is just nagging and trying to spoil your fun! You always have the means to justify your actions. What attraction do these things hold for you? I have heard spouses responding to their beloved in this vein: "That is why I do not come home" or "And you expect me to come home when you are talking like that?" Get real and grow up! You are not doing each other a favour by being committed to one another! You are both responsible for the success of your marriage. Each of you needs to invest 100 percent of all you are and all you have into this marriage. Change the mentality that says the other person has been vested with the capacity or capability to do a greater part. A marriage is more than a vow at the altar; it is a promise made with God as a witness that is fulfilled with a vow to emotional, psychological and lifelong commitment. You cannot afford to be casual about it.

You must not forget that both of you are on the same side; you are fighting a battle against a common enemy—the devil—not against each other. So, you need to unite and kick out of your lives anything that seeks to ruin your marriage. Strategize if you have not done so already. Determine to be a strong force and be aware that you have committed to a lifelong journey together. *No quitting!* The fight and fun have just begun! Be a united force, committed to one another, and nothing can break or destroy your bond. Because now you have an ally, you are well-positioned. You have your spouse and the Almighty God by your side. The battle must be won!

You are on the right team—the winning one! This is a very conscious choice or decision couples must make. Being emotionally, psychologically and lifelong committed would mean here that you are willing to give up your freedom and choices that would otherwise seek to become hindrances in your home. I am not trying to say that because you are married, you need to lose your individuality and become just a shadow of yourself. You cannot just always go leaving your spouse behind! You might have professed undying love for one another and thought this was all you needed for your marriage to be successful. After all, you just need to love each other, and your spouse already knows you love her/him; the rest is just a piece of cake.

Well, the truth is that marriage needs hard work. It transcends what you see in movies or read in the pages of your romance novels where a girl is swept off her feet by a guy on bended knee. She says, "I do" and they get married and live happily ever after. Ooh! We love this! However, we are not shown the other part that says, "After *I do* comes the hard work!" Our heads are filled with the notion that it is going to be smooth sailing all along.

You hear people often asking how he proposed, how did you respond, and what happened when you said yes, but no one bothers or pauses to contemplate what happens after this. Some of you weave lavish dreams around this day and the wedding. So, you do everything within your power to see that he proposes. Then the craze sets in! You start planning a very glamorous wedding with bells and whistles and all the trappings. You just stop where the wedding is solemnized, and you throw your bouquet to your friends and zoom off! What a beautiful wedding; you smile secretly to yourself. Your dream has been fulfilled; you have finally done it!

You go into marriage for the wrong reasons. There are various reasons why people go into marriage. What was yours? Some are just looking for a father or mother they never had, while others might be looking for security in one way or another. So, it is no wonder that at the first sign of anything that does not conform to your ideology of marriage, you are out the door. How has such an honourable union been reduced to this level? It is now almost like kids playing house! Why get married if you have no vested interest in it?

All that matters is that he/she planned something romantic and impressed the girl or boy. When the guy pops the question, he has a basic understanding of what marriage is in his mind; after all, he has seen the display countless times in movies and intends for it to last a lifetime, as most people who enter into marriage do. Divorce is the last thought on their minds as they love each other so dearly. That is bound to be the deciding factor for marriage, is it not? They are sure this is guaranteed to be successful and will last a lifetime. Have you paused for a minute to ask yourselves if you are ready to be husband and wife to each other? Do you know what you are getting into? Are you really committed to doing the work that is required to make this union successful? Okay!

Except you are willing to commit emotionally, psychologically and lifelong and take a long breath and decide to put in the work that is needed, you will be in for a long boring, unfulfilling, tedious and substandard married life. The romantic proposal and big fat wedding party with all the bells and whistles will fly out the window as they mean nothing to you at this period. Trust me, when you get to the point where you have forgotten the simple pleasures you had in your life, there is no way you will remember or think of the good things God has in store for you or what He can do for you in your life and marriage if you could only turn to Him. There are absolutely no guarantees in life, and neither are there any in marriage, for as the Bible states in James 4:13–15:

> Now listen, you who say, "Today or tomorrow we will go to this or that city, spend a year there, carry on

> business and make money." Why, you
> do not even know what will happen
> tomorrow. What is your life? You are
> a mist that appears for a little while
> and then vanishes. Instead, you ought
> to say, "If it is the Lord's will, we will
> live and do this or that."

Well, what are waiting for? Do not be fools and think you have all the time in the world! Make the best of your marriage! Stop the mind games and manipulation! You are only sure of the now, so make the best of it and live your lives to the fullest, being committed to each other while also pleasing the Lord and not the flesh! Forget the movies, glossy magazines, and books. Don't just go with the flow— decide to be emotionally, psychologically and lifelong committed to your spouse and marriage. For there is no perfect time as now for true commitment. Remember how important it was for you to make the vows you made to each other in front of God and witnesses. They sounded so passionate and romantic even to the onlookers as you promised to live together until one of you dies, no matter what might happen. To share both sorrows and joys, poverty and plenty, sickness and health. Is the commitment still of the same importance to you?

I cannot help but emphasize that the best thing you can do for yourselves is to understand right from the onset that marriage requires hard work. Both husband

and wife must invest 100 percent, not 50 percent of their time, themselves, and all that the marriage needs to make it work into it. Note here that I said *must!* It is not conditional if you want a successful marriage. In marriage, you have no option but to have the Lord as the head and to keep working on it! You cannot be selfish and entitled in this relationship. This is because you are used to demanding your individual rights in the society you live in. This attitude does not work well in marriage as the reverse is the case. You are both important members of this union.

Therefore, in marriage, two people who lived only for themselves now must learn to put their spouse's needs above their own, be dedicated to another person, and stay true to a relationship. The mere idea of this is enough to cause a lot of grief, leaving a lot of people feeling trapped and bewildered. Their first impulse is to shun marriage and all it represents, playing right into the devil's hands. He wants you to fail and he tries everything possible to see you do just that! Your response when marriage is mentioned is to run or be noncommittal about it. You must resolve to be faithful and really mean it. It is just not enough for you to say you are and your words do not correlate with your actions.

Note that before adultery takes place, you have an opportunity to see and choose to go ahead with whatever impulse controls you. Marriage demands that both spouses be faithful and trust each other. You cannot be committed to someone if you do not trust them. If it is the case of lack of trust, remember that both of you went into marriage with certain expectations and understanding. When your trust is broken or suspicion arises due to some reason, realize that you have a right to stop, talk, and evaluate what is going on with your spouse. Do not try the silent treatment. Because both of you are married, you have every right to hold each other accountable. Confront one another when the need arises as this helps in building character and one another up. Proverbs 27:5-6 says:

> Better is open rebuke than love that
> is concealed.
>
> Faithful are the wounds of a friend, but
> deceitful are the kisses of an enemy.

Talk and work it out together until the trust is rebuilt. If something is bothering you, put in efforts to talk this out with your spouse because if you do not do so how do you expect your spouse to read what is going on in your mind? However, it takes more than words to help in rebuilding trust as it is not earned by words only but by consistent deed, prayer, action, and a lot of patience. Some of you just wait for the opportunity for betrayal to happen so you can just walk out of the relationship. I have heard a lot of people say, "I am just biding my time and waiting for when he does something to annoy me this time and

I will just walk out!" What commitment! Are they really invested in their marriages? I know that no matter what happens if you resolve to make it work and exercise some patience while you take it to the Lord in prayer, He will renew your heart, spouse, and relationship.

Commit your ways to the Lord and be confident of the spouse he has given to you because He will surely direct your path. You live in a world where you have a lot of options at your disposal. There is no better time than now for you to throw away all options at your disposal but that of success. Success only comes through the Lord. Remember, marriage is not a testing arena; once you get into it, it should be for life. Resist the urge to indulge in making decisions without consulting your spouse. Talk to each other about even the smallest thing that concerns your marriage. Men, I urge you not to be in a rush to dismiss what your spouse says as God has given both of you great wisdom to be able to counsel each other. Always bear in mind that God has put them in your lives to also correct and edify you in love.

The heart of her husband trusts in her and he will have no lack of gain. She does him good and not evil all the days of her life. Strength and dignity are her clothing, and she smiles at the future. She opens her mouth in wisdom, and the teaching of kindness is on her tongue. She looks well to the ways of her household and does not eat the bread of idleness. Thus, she makes a home where husband and children like to be. Her children rise up and bless her; her husband also, and he praises her.

—Proverbs 31:11–12; 25–28

Chapter Nine

Trio: Wife, Husband ...God

The Bible says in Psalm 127:1, "Unless the LORD builds the house, the builders labor in vain. Unless the LORD watches over the city, the guards stand watch in vain." And we see in Leviticus 26:20 that "your strength will be spent in vain. For your land will not yield its produce, and the trees of the land will not bear their fruit."

Our homes are no less than vineyards. They need to be watered, nourished, pruned, and cared for so we can have a bountiful harvest. The Bible tells us that anything we do without God at the centre cannot flourish. Marriage is very important, and it is only fitting that we should have the Creator at its head so that we do not toil or labour in vain and our efforts are not wasted.

With God at the centre of our marriages, we can all have very happy homes and successful marriages. It all begins with God! Everything we set our sights on begins with God! Bearing this in mind, we must commit all our affairs to God and watch how He turns everything to our favour!

Do you want a successful marriage, career, success in the small and big affairs in your lives? Just turn it all to Him and He will never let you down. God must be at the forefront of every marriage for it to succeed. This is because being the Creator and maker of the marriage institution and everything on Earth, He holds the key to a marriage's success. If He instituted marriage, then who would be in the best position to help unravel the mysteries of our lives and the insecurities that might arise concerning marriage? As with all ranges of inventions or machinery we buy or acquire in the world, it is common knowledge that, whenever you have a problem with your product, be it mechanical or electronic, what is the first step you follow? You look for the owner's manual so you can troubleshoot to get it back in working order. If this fails, you immediately go back to where you got it or send it back to the manufacturer so the problem can be fixed.

So, what makes the difference when it comes to our lives or it concerns marriage? Why do we find it so difficult to take matters to Him for some troubleshooting? Why are we so reluctant? He demands nothing outrageous from us. He loves us unconditionally! A relationship with Him is glorious and reviving. It is free of charge and He knows how best to solve our problems and would do anything to make our marriages successful.

He knows best how He wants this to operate. He has the blueprint for all marriages. The first question to ask ourselves here is, do you know Him? He holds the key to your success in His hand and He helps you make the right choices concerning your children, husband, wife, and even the little things you feel are not important to Him.

A careful look at creation would immediately show you what our situation is to be like! You see valleys, mountains, plains, flatland, and so forth. There is diversity revealed in creation. This on its own should denote to you that we are on a walk with God, be it in our careers, businesses, marriages, etc. God designed it in such a way that there will be lows and highs, different stages that all meld together to make our lives lush, rich, and fulfilling. This is so that you would not lose sight of what is important in your lives! Seeking and glorifying the Almighty! It is often the case that, when everything seems to be going too well in our lives, we tend to forget how we got there, who made it so, and sometimes become too proud and give the glory to ourselves or to something else.

The bumps on the way as lows, or the detours and setbacks, bring back your focus to the central figure: *God!* It is necessary that when you hit your lows or highs, you call upon Him to stabilize you as He never makes mistakes. A marriage that is formed with God as the central figure, not friends and relatives, is the ultimate one. Counsel from friends and others is welcome but can so often mislead you, while a word from the Lord can never set you on the wrong path.

Most people run to friends and relatives who give them advice that is supposedly tried and tested, and it is backed by their guarantee to work! You do not need to lap up their advice because you are not them, and what worked for them might not necessarily work for you. Doing what they ask you to anyway is for their own good, so they become your legal and illegal advisers. If by some fluke, there is a slight shift in your circumstances due to their counsel, the praise immediately is ascribed to their wisdom! Bear in mind that, on the contrary, it is these very people who are out to distort and destroy your home. The Bible has the following to say: "I am the LORD; that is my name! I will not give my glory to anyone else, nor share my praise with carved idols" (Isaiah 42:8).

Permit me to make this clear: I am not in any way discouraging you from seeking counsel but be careful whom you go to. If possible, do some research to see that the advice given is based on the precepts set out by the Lord before putting them to use. Use Christian leaders who are living fulfilled and God-fearing lives. I am saying this because I have had cases where breakups happened just because some advice was given by someone who knew little or nothing about God's intention for marriage, and it led to a whole lot of trouble! In short, unknown to this couple, their counsellor was going through greater crises in his home. Without the divine intervention of God through another person, they would have had one of the dirtiest divorces recorded!

From experience, I have seen people weave webs of lies just because they felt threatened or intimidated by the success of their friends' relationships, or since theirs was not working, they might as well also destroy their friends. As they say, misery loves company. Why build your home trying to fulfill another person's desires when he never should have a say in it? It is time to pull the wool from your eyes and be the best friend and spouse you can ever be to each other! So if we are paying close attention to what the Bible says, it is then mandatory for all husbands to frequently examine themselves to see where they are failing to be the provider, lover, friend, etc. their wives need them to be, and God commands them to be. You have been created in God's image and are not wayward, gullible, easily deceived, nor foolish. God made you good and more than enough. Honour God with every aspect of your lives and stop making excuses. If you are in any way unwise, get wisdom. Seek the Lord.

Being husbands, you need to find ways to love your wives with Christ-like love. Need I remind you here that marriage is not just a private happening, no matter how personal you thought your relationship was, even when you were dating. Now you are married and accountable to not only each other, but both of you are accountable to God for the past, present, and future of your marriage. The choices and decisions you make are not only going to affect you as a couple but your children and future generations. This is the time to remember that the welfare of the coming generations is also involved. What you do matters more than you know. It is then necessary that the husband rises and takes his rightful place in the home as a husband, friend, provider, protector, and father. He must give guidance to his wife and children, bear the household responsibility, take the initiative, and with gentleness and courage, encourage and aid his wife in becoming all the Lord has created her to be. When a woman feels appreciated and loved, she can fight any demon that threatens the welfare of her family and home.

A wife who feels encouraged by her husband can rise to any situation and do wonders for the home and her community. The more a husband stands in his truth, performs his duty as a husband and has the support of his wife who is a friend, because she is wife and nurturer, the more affectionate, strong, and warm the bond of marriage becomes and remains.

As both couples perform their roles, the wife becomes a real help as she pays great attention to her household and creates a "home." Proverbs 31:11–12, 25–28 states that because of this woman of virtue:

> The heart of her husband trusts in her and he will have no lack of gain. She does him good and not evil all the

days of her life. Strength and dignity are her clothing, and she smiles at the future. She opens her mouth in wisdom, and the teaching of kindness is on her tongue. She looks well to the ways of her household and does not eat the bread of idleness. Thus, she makes a home where husband and children like to be…. Her children rise up and bless her; her husband also, and he praises her.

Who does not want a happy home with well-rounded children?

You are in a relationship with your spouse, not on the battleground! I have heard stories of husbands who are quick to raise their hands to their wives when they disagree. Excuse me here. I think this is not only disrespectful and demeaning but should never be condoned in the home. If you are in dire need of a punching bag, may I suggest you find yourself a very good gymnasium and become a member? You know what would work best? Buy a punching bag so you can have it where and when you need it—your home! No one was made to be thrown around. If your spouse holds any value for you, you will never think of hurting them. Do not forget that it is only where husband and wife demonstrate the image of Christ that they will then learn to deny themselves. Bury their selfish nature and like Christ, they will also learn to love and serve each other in the true sense.

True love knows no bounds and you should accept the other person with all his or her foibles, peculiarities, weaknesses, pettiness, and even their strengths. We were created to celebrate each other's differences, walk together in fellowship, companionship, mutual respect, and affection. When there is true acceptance, then this will make a way for love to prepare a home for the other. Marriage and the family will then provide a resting place, a natural haven from the unpredictable and hectic pace of the outside and modern life. The wife who is loved selflessly and valued makes the home habitable and pleasant, a haven for the husband, children, and other family members to come to at the end of the day.

The environment in the home will not be strained nor artificial as these manners will be unnecessary at home. You are free to be you. This is one place you can be without feeling judged or have the need to put up any barriers because true love knows that your spouse is not without human frailties nor failures, and you are accepted just as you are. It does not compare the other with or to an ideal lest one disillusionment after the other set in. Love alone endures all things. Faults and imperfections exist in all of us and will be seen in love. As a result, you must accept your partner as given by God for life and not a clone of someone from the glossy pages of the magazines or the ivory screen of the television.

When a wife understands that her husband loves, cherishes, respects, holds her in high esteem, and surrounds her with care and attention, she will immediately blossom. She will perform her duty with love and happiness, bringing joy, peace, and happiness to the home. Mutual affection, respect, love, and joy will be maintained and strengthened. Nothing then can stop love from flourishing in the home despite how busy the household is, and no matter how many large or small irritations and storms seek to tear it down.

This relationship is supposed to be a dance of two hearts. Always ask yourself the reason why you got married and remember the promises you have made to each other. What has happened to change your perspective? I will suggest you retrace your steps and seek the help of the Lord to find where you lost yourselves along the way.

You need to understand that nothing is as deadly as the little three-letter word: *ego!* It can burn fiercer than any raging wildfire and can also destroy nations. Due to this, some men can hardly bring themselves to lend a helping hand to their spouses when the need arises. Work toward helping each other. When facing difficulty, do not let your lack of forgiveness turn into resentment and then give reign to the ego! Do not give this villain the opportunity to dictate to you how to treat your spouse. It does not deserve your consideration in the slightest. You are better than that. Fight like you have never done before to make your marriages work! Save your marriage because nothing is worth giving it up for.

As husband and wife, consult each other on things that affect both of you and your family. Trust one another. Men, note that God's purpose for creating women was so that you would be each other's companion, one in purpose, heart, and one as well in the physical union. To make this union beautiful, start by casting your cares unto the Lord! He will direct you on how to show support and display trust for the one you have sworn to love, no matter how believable the lies you are being told sound or look. Be warned that things are not always as they seem because there are always two sides to a coin. As they say, "All that glitters is not gold!"

The foundation of all marriages should be God, and then trust, companionship, friendship, and love. God should be at the forefront of your marriage. As the Bible says in Matthew 6:33, "But seek first his kingdom and his righteousness, and all these things will be given to you as well."

This is because love alone in most cases, as construed by man, is fickle and most often cannot stand the test of time. When you take the time to cultivate friendship and companionship, on the other hand, these are long-standing. As mentioned in the Bible in Proverbs 18:24: "One who has unreliable friends soon comes to ruin: but there is a friend that sticks closer than a brother."

Most marriages fall apart not because there is a lack of love but because most couples never take the pains to understand and relate with each other as friends. If the concept of true friendship and understanding operates in a marriage, couples work their differences out rather than take the easy way out. If you leave an exit door open in marriage, the opportunity to use it will definitely present itself one day. So be careful and align your values for success.

Sometimes lust is mistaken for love. And when the blinders come off, we realize that it was just an infatuation; it cannot stand the test of time. It feels suddenly like you have just woken up from deep slumber and you can now see clearly. But it is a little too late now to think it through! Hello, you are now a married woman/man!

Friends have no barriers to hold them back. They can express themselves easily and sincerely. They have no hidden agenda except the fact that they love each other and enjoy spending time together. True friends do not care about beauty. Give each other the opportunity to be the best of friends and get to know each other before moving ahead. When you decide to get married, be sure to lead side by side. The husbands should lead as husbands and the women should support and help them as women. Always pray together and know or identify who your enemy is. Love one another and determine to stand for what is true and what you believe in.

Husbands to love their wives just as Christ also loved the Church and gave himself for her.

—Ephesians 5:25

Submission

The word *submission* should not evoke images of slavery or inferiority toward the one who is submissive. As defined by the dictionary, *submission* is the act of accepting or yielding to a superior force or to the will or authority of another person. It is often a mandatory or obligatory requirement, and it is the act of submitting to or being under the authority or control of someone or something else. As human beings, we always try to find ways of not submitting or rebelling against this authority. As enjoined by the Bible, if you want a happy and successful marriage, you have no choice but to submit.

Therefore, submission as portrayed in the Bible in 1 Peter 3:4–6 states:

> Rather, it should be that of your inner self, the unfading beauty of a gentle and quiet spirit, which is of

great worth in God's sight. For this is the way the holy women of the past who put their hope in God used to adorn themselves. They submitted themselves to their own husbands, like Sarah, who obeyed Abraham and called him her lord. You are her daughters if you do what is right and do not give way to fear.

Most of you read this and the first thought is, "I am not even going to give that a second thought because that was the Old Testament and Sarah needed to do that, not me!" In this era where roles are swapped, men most often have abdicated their positions of authority as they have failed to be the heads. Some, just for peace to reign in the home, have suddenly lost their voices and position of authority. I must confess that it is a marital mistake for a wife and husband not to be submissive to one another. Paul calls for submission in Ephesians 5:21 by saying thus: "Submitting yourselves one to another in the fear of God." He also stated that there is no difference in status between a man and a woman. As stated in Galatians 3:28, "There is neither Jew nor Gentile, neither slave nor free, nor is there male and female, for you are all one in Christ Jesus."

We must understand the woman's commission as outlined in the Bible. Due to the many wrong interpretations given to the topic of submission, couples are living in relationships where they are not able to fulfill their God-given roles. Some see the concept of submission as an insult. This was not the intention. Submission is first and foremost God's idea; it is an instruction given by Him that is meant to facilitate teamwork in the family so there is no confusion as couples strive for the betterment of the home. God did this to eliminate the chaos that could arise from two people trying to be at the helm of affairs in the home. We can only imagine how this would be! So, it makes absolute sense that as working partners, there should be one helpmeet. It is God's way of saying that there cannot be two captains in a ship nor two presidents at the same time in a country; one must step down for the other to take over the reins of government.

The wife is to follow the example set by Christ for the church. She must submit totally to her husband. As a woman/wife, when you obey God and submit to your husband, you unleash the blessings of obedience as promised by God, and these then become your lot. We see this promise in Isaiah 1:9 stating that "the good of the land will only flow to the willing and obedient woman." I know that as a woman, I want my home to be happy and I will obey any command with such an authentic promise backed by the Almighty as displayed above.

Can we just pause for a while and take another look at this promise? Your submission is not only necessary, but it opens the goodness of the land, which will only flow into the home because of the obedient woman. Your submission to your husband is so powerful that even your prayers for your husbands are answered because you are walking in obedience. Progress will be recorded as shown in Genesis 11:6. Nothing you plan as couples will be impossible for you as you enjoy the benefits of working in unity and agreement. You are working in sync; nothing will, therefore, be difficult to accomplish. This is because when a woman submits, the kingdom of God is portrayed in the light, and God is glorified.

Apart from the fact that when you submit, you glorify God, your marriage will flourish as your submission serves as a trigger to your husband's understanding and submission. He begins to see you as an inseparable and vital part of him. The beauty of it is that you are on the same page as your spouse as you work together toward building your home. We walk in ignorance and do not realize that, as a mandate from God, submission is mutual and necessary, and it is vital that both parties conform to this. So, if you have not been submissive, now is the time for you to take steps to submit today and watch how God begins to glorify Himself in your life.

When I talk about submission, I always get an emphatic, *"Oh no!* Do not go there because that is one thing I cannot do. I am no one's slave." This reaction is not new. I always get it from people who feel they should fight for their rights and prove to their husbands that they are as good as them, if not better. While the husbands, on the other hand, think it is not their duty to submit. When we understand what God wants of us, we can embrace this command wholeheartedly.

May I point out here that by submission, God does not mean you should become a slave to your husband nor vice versa. God, in His mercy and love, would not create us to be abused or bullied. Trust me, this is the greatest power and divine enablement both of you possess to win over your husband or wife. When you submit as a woman and your husband understands this, things begin to happen in your marriage and your lives. There is greater intimacy, understanding, and love. It would not be wrong to say that this is because of having obeyed the Lord's command. The roles in the home are not swapped, and each person is fulfilling their responsibility.

A quick look at the Bible shows that Sarah called Abraham "Lord." You might be tempted to ask where the crown was. It was in the heart and the knowledge that God demanded this of her. Or, aha! Why should you do this? Your husband is in no way superior to you! Calm down here! I am not talking once more about the war of the sexes, but have you ever wondered why God in all His wisdom enjoined man to love his wife and the wife to be submissive? That is because men and women have different needs to be fulfilled. They are wired differently. A man cannot become a woman, neither can a woman become a man, no matter what your job title, wealth, or rank! If this happens, there is bound to be some discrepancies or maladjustment.

I am not trying to say that a woman is incapable of doing what a man does! Of course, the reverse is the case here. Women are so well endowed that they can rise and take up any challenge they want to in the society or home. We must not, however, be deceived into thinking that, because of our accomplishments, we have suddenly become the men in the house. One thing, though, remains constant: We must fulfill our roles as wives at the end of the day. Not doing this would be going contrary to the dictates of the Bible.

Be cognizant of the fact that you, as a woman, are part of something bigger. So, when you decide to get married, you have been empowered to work alongside your husband to bring glory to the Lord. There are certain promises God can bring to pass only when husbands and wives live passionately together, not just coexisting but are committed to their calling as couples. Be committed to working together so that God will bless your unity. Realize that because man and woman are created differently, this difference can then be used in complementing one another rather than tearing each other apart. Paul in the Bible enjoined women to be submissive and "husbands to love their wives just as Christ also loved the church and gave himself for her" (Ephesians 5:25). He also added that both should submit to each other in the fear of God (Ephesians 5:21). It is the husband's responsibility *as* head of the family to fulfill all religious duties in the home, like taking the family to church or making sure that all religious ordinances are obeyed in the home. He is to coach the children, and teach them the faith, to examine the whole family after each sermon, to see how much has been retained and understood, and to fill any gaps in their understanding that might remain, to lead the family in worship daily, ideally twice a day, and to set an example of sober godliness always and in all matters. The husband must be willing to take time out to learn the faith that he is charged to teach.

God has established the authority structure that should operate in a Christian home where marriage is honoured and the marital bed is kept holy. The Bible in Galatians 3:28 and 1 Corinthians 11:11–12 states that as Christians, men and women are equal. They have both been created to tend the earth God has made, and as a result, there is no difference in their standing with God. From my experience in life, it is sometimes the case that some women are better in terms of intelligence, understanding, and various other gifts than their husbands. However, in the Christian home, there is a hierarchy that has been instituted. The man is under Christ, the woman is under her husband's authority, and the children are under the authority of their parents.

Nowhere is it inferred that one is to be superior to the other. Instead, what we can see here is an admonition that will bring about greater unity in the home. Each person has a different niche or role to play.

It is not the relationship between master and slave but that of two equals working toward the fulfillment of a common goal—the success of the home/marriage; resulting in a very fruitful, successful, and happy marriage. Men and women are different because they each have different emotional needs that are to be filled and taken into consideration. Men have an innate need to feel respected by their wives, and when this need is met, a husband will go to any lengths to keep his wife happy. The role of the head of the house comes into play automatically as he feels respected and very confident in fulfilling his role. Do you still wonder why you should be submissive toward your husband?

Women need to feel loved by their husbands. When a woman feels loved, everything changes in the home. She guards her home with all dedication and makes sure everyone is happy. She glows, and this happiness spills over to everyone and everything she does. This was the reason Paul gave the specific instructions the way he did. We turn a deaf ear to what the Bible enjoins us to do in our bid to assert ourselves as the superior party in the relationship. A wife submits because of her reverence for Christ (Ephesians 5:22), not because she is a slave or inferior to her husband. This demonstrates her acceptance of and obedience to God's instructions concerning marriage and the church. The wife is to follow the example set by Christ for the church. Wives must submit totally to their husbands in everything. Both have been assigned significant and different roles in the family and in the church. None is more superior to the other.

Husbands are to love their wives just as Christ loved the church, whereby He demonstrated it by dying on the cross (Ephesians 5:25) so that the wife can become pure and holy without stain. Let us pause for a moment here and take in what the Bible is saying about the husband's love for his wife! So, can we assume that there is a condition for the wife's purity here? Is it possible that the husband's love or lack of love for his wife can affect the wife? Therefore, for the wife to be holy, the husband needs to love her just as Christ loved the church, even unto giving His life up for it! I would assume here that, husbands, as you get into marriage with your wives, your intention is for you to have a very happy marriage! You want your wives to be pure and holy! You would not hesitate to give your lives up for them. If you are living lives as prescribed by the Bible, then why do we have more unhappy wives than is necessary?

The problem here is that we are not invested in marriages as we have been directed to be. The self is still very much in control of all of you. Your thinking is still about what would please you as an individual and bring you happiness, not what would bring about happiness for you as a couple. It boils down to just what you want. I hear couples saying things like, "I just need to think about me here, you know?" Well, how do you only think about you when you are on the journey of becoming *one*? Remember, this love transcends sexual love and even friendship. It is sacrificial for the one it loves. You have to first experience the love of Christ before you can express this love to your spouse. This is the only time you can die to the self and love as you were meant to.

Husbands, you are to love your wives sacrificially despite imperfections, just as Christ did the church. Jesus loved us, although He knew what we would do. He regarded us as friends despite our sinful nature. He looked past our sins and still loved us. If you want a godly home, you can honour and teach the gospel in your home so that your wife becomes Christ-like through this love. The norm in most homes is that most husbands have abdicated their thrones and left the wives to play both roles of husband and wives. In Hebrews 13:4, we are told that we should also serve God acceptably in our marriages. Christians have no freedom to live their married lives for their own pleasure. Our married lives should be consecrated for the glory of God. Husbands, you are to love and treat your wives with the same care that you would your bodies. Ephesians 5:28–29 says:

> In this same way, husbands ought to love their wives as their own bodies. He who loves his wife loves himself. After all, no one ever hated their own body, but they feed and care for their body, just as Christ does the church.

Through the wife's submission to the husband's leadership, the husband gains insight on how he ought to trust Christ and submit to His leadership. As the husband seeks to make his wife holy, the wife gains insight into the depths of God's love for her. These are the ingredients for oneness in marriage. As each of you understands and fulfills your individual roles, you gain deeper insights into what it means to be one with God. This is a little heaven on Earth! If someone wanted to know what heaven is like, they could be directed to your home.

If the devil can ruin the home, he can ruin society, making it worse with each passing generation. We can see this in the immorality and sexual pervasion that has riddled our society. The Lord has given us a reason to be hopeful. Isaiah 59:19 says, "When the enemy shall come in like a flood, the Spirit of the LORD shall lift up a standard against him." Entrust your homes to God, and He will keep them safe from the clutches of the devil. Make sure you maintain the laid-down standards for Christian living. It is the standard of godly homes. And it begins with godly marriages. Strive together to make your family one that God can use to be a standard against the flood that the devil is pouring on the world. Commit your ways to the Lord God, and He will help you as husbands and wives to build godly families.

By wisdom a house is built, and by understanding it is established; by knowledge the rooms are filled with all precious and pleasant riches.

—Proverbs 24:3–4

Finances

One of the most annoying and puzzling things that can happen to you is to look at life and wonder why you always work hard and never seem to have enough! You must manage your finances and wonder if others need to do the same. It looks like you were just made to work while others can afford to live luxurious lives, eat where they want to, drive all the flashy cars they want, and above all still have a lot of money left to squander! You tell yourself life is not fair! Why can't you ever have more than enough? Why do you slug and toil all the time and still not make ends meet? An idea hits you! You could start stashing some money away; after all, what your spouse does not know would not hurt her/him, would it? What you do not know is that doing this will come back to bite you! No matter the financial problems you are going through, this is a very bad idea! What is the need that cannot be shared with your spouse so that you can find a solution together? Who are you saving the money for?

Are there needs you have that are hidden from your spouse? Remember, you are on the same team. What affects you affects him. So, it is not a bad idea to sit down and have a heart-to-heart talk instead of resorting to this. The chances are if he/she says no, then you are obviously not in dire need of what you are trying to stash cash away for. If it is a personal need, still try to discuss this with your spouse and see what his/her thoughts are. Please do not resort to cheating! It can be destructive and belittling too. Talking about your concerns will help you achieve a closer and deeper relationship with your spouse. You would also understand better what vantage point you are working from.

You are a gift from God to one another. When you dishonour each other, you dishonour God. Stashing away cash dishonours your spouse. When discussing money matters at home, use this avenue to teach, correct, and edify or encourage one another, not humiliate. If there is a point of discord, find a humble and honourable way to express your anger. Do not resort to shouting and using below-the-belt tactics. You might have had the last word, but that does not mean you have won.

A very old friend came in to see me looking all worried and crestfallen. She did not know where to start her tale of woe. All she could say was that she was tired. On further discussion, she broke down and confessed that her husband had accused her of being insensitive, reckless, greedy, and careless. I learned that he had given her money for shopping that morning and expected her to give him a breakdown of everything she had spent to the letter. She could not do this, and he launched into a tirade of abuses. She felt so insulted and disrespected that she could not help but burst into tears and run out the door. She came straight to me. I must confess she was a pack of nerves and extremely angry. I invite you to take a quick look at the expletives, and you can see that these are not words you should use on your spouse, even if she robbed your bank!

How would you feel if the tables were turned and you were subjected to this treatment? Remember the Golden Rule? "Do unto others what you want others to do unto you!" I am not disputing the importance of keeping good records of the household expenditures because even the Bible says, "By wisdom a house is built, and by understanding it is established; by knowledge the rooms are filled with all precious and pleasant riches" (Proverbs 24:3–4). This is very simple and clear as couples can't have their finances under control unless they understand the basics of good record-keeping. However, it should not suddenly be because it concerns money that you have forgotten that though you are two individuals, you have become one. What hurts her should hurt you and you are not to insult nor trample her self-respect and dignity! Especially not because of money! Have you become the abhorred principal and your spouse the recalcitrant pupil?

When we look carefully at situations like these, it is easy to realize that most disputes over money are a battle for power and supremacy. This is often the case where one partner tries to stamp or reinforce his position as the superior one because he earns most of the income. A good leader is not a dictator but one who listens calmly and tries to resolve matters without resorting to bullying or conflict. Some of you become real-life Scrooges when matters of money are raised in the home. You have the greatest reasons for not giving to a cause that is not directly connected to you. Are we not forgetting something here? You are one! If only you could have the same reaction toward yourself when it comes to spending this same money! There are always reasons why you need to do certain things, but these do not apply to your spouse. The Bible has this to say:

> Here is a trustworthy saying: Whoever aspires to be an overseer desires a noble task. Now the overseer is to be above reproach, faithful to his wife, temperate, self-controlled, respectable, hospitable, able to teach, not given to drunkenness, not violent but gentle, not quarrelsome, not a lover of money. He must manage his own family well and see that his children obey

him, and he must do so in a manner worthy of full respect. (If anyone does not know how to manage his own family, how can he take care of God's church?) (1Timothy 3:1–5)

If you continue disrespecting your spouse, you are not only putting a strain on your relationship but driving away any intimacy between you. Both of you must agree on your finances and how to resolve such discrepancies in your home. It is not a sign of being inferior if the wife yields to her husband and allows the Lord to work it out. As they work together, encouraging one another, God will show them His favour and grace. Nevertheless, being responsible as the leader does not mean the husband should become a dictator or lord and master whose word is final. The couple should discuss and agree on financial management.

Every home needs a sensitive, discerning wife as she is a great asset to any husband if he's willing to listen to her. Husbands, note, however, that the burden of maintaining a trouble-free, financially sound, spiritually mature, and cooperatively considerate household is your responsibility, which can be seen in the Bible in 1 Timothy 3:4–5. Let us not forget that it is the wife's responsibility to support her husband and honour him by following his direction. We know that as women, we find it easier to nag and belittle our husbands and make them feel they are not doing as much as they should. This is not the right way to go. You should be willing to support your husband.

If both of you are not well-versed in financial management, please get educated. It will save you a lot of trouble. I am saying this because my husband and I ran into a lot of trouble when we trusted our finances to the "expert management of our very capable accountant," whom we felt had our best interest at heart! It took the grace of God to get us out of this debacle and help us realize we were being set up and used. We thank God for delivering us from this disaster that was about to strike. As the Bible says, "The simple believes everything, but the prudent gives thought to his steps" (Proverbs 14:15). Most financially naive couples, as we were, are not stupid regarding money; we were just naive and uninformed regarding how accounting and the tax system worked. Our primary concern was how to get these done. So, we felt we just needed the help of someone knowledgeable to help us through this. Permit me to mention that he came with great recommendations from people we knew and respected, but almost became our worst nightmare if it had not been for God's grace and intervention! You would be surprised to know how many people fall into such traps due to a lack of knowledge. Be careful not to become one of them.

When you experience financial crises, you go on overdrive and start trying to fix things. You are sure that if you and your spouse could just work a little harder on things, you might be able to live like you have always imagined or even better. If you are in a single-income home, you start feeling discontented! You wonder why your spouse cannot help you a little. I am not saying anything is wrong with wanting your spouse to contribute or help you make money for the home! But have you surrendered this problem to the Lord? Okay, take a pause and look around you and see what the Lord has blessed you with! It is now time to cast your burdens upon Him and see what He will do for you. It is a known fact that the number one cause of divorce and quarrels in marriage is money. This is because your decisions are no longer based on God's principles but on the self and your egos. You think you have got everything figured out! The Bible says they labour in vain whose foundation is not on the Lord. This is because it would have imperfections. (There are a lot of imperfections and most of us know how to look for them.) It often takes just a little nudge for you to fish them out, then you proceed to blow everything out of proportion! Well, hello, who doesn't have them? If we were without any, we would not be on this planet. Quit the blame game and rise up, seek the Lord, and work as a team. Do not hide money, do not hide debt, and be considerate toward one another.

The Family

Ruth allowed her circumstances to define her after the death of her husband and children. She felt she had no reason to live anymore. She got to the stage where she lost all hope!

The truth is that when a man and woman come together in marriage, they are not going into an island to be alone. They are from two very different extended families comprising of different values—sometimes different cultures and traditions, and even different social statuses. Most of these differences can be as clear as chalk from clay or as far apart as the east is to the west. These differences have been known to be troublesome and can bring undue pressure to the newly married.

It is always the case that when the families are not well-balanced in status, class, or affluence, the more affluent family exhibits snobbish behaviour toward the other family. The affluent family can be rude, aggressive, or downright condescending. I cannot overemphasize the effect the pressure, possessive expectations, and demands from in-laws and extended families can inflict on the married couple or newlyweds who may already be strained in their bid to establish a family, plan for children, develop careers, and cope with financial obligations. So, my question here is, how do couples deal with this? It is not helpful to realize that our world now lauds single-family units with people going into marriages hoping to live just by themselves so they can forget their parents! Just forget about them and live your lives on your own terms. After all, there are a lot of homes to cater to them! Is it possible for you to just throw or cast them aside and pretend they are not there? Do we pander to the wishes of the more dominant couple and ignore the lesser ones? The Bible in 1 Timothy 5:8 has this to say: "Anyone who does not provide for their relatives, and especially for their own household, has denied the faith and is worse than an unbeliever."

One of the reasons why this conflict arises in the first place is because of our set patterns and mindset. When I was newly married, my husband and I shared a home with my parents-in-law and sisters-in-law and their families. I had a lot of people advise me to pick a fight with my husband so we could move to our own home. Their reason was that they knew I was not going to be treated well by my in-laws and they felt it was my right to demand that I would not stand for it.

Unbeknownst to them, I had gone into marriage with my mind made up that his people were going to be my people. I was not being controlled by the spirit of Ruth in the Bible. I was just resolute to do the right thing as I needed peace in my home. So, if I respected my parents and siblings, I was going to do just the same for his family. I was not going to feel bad if I was corrected for a mistake I made but be gracious enough to apologize and work toward correcting it if possible. The advice kept coming and, to their surprise, we made no move to move after more than four years in the same home, even though we had enough money to buy our own home and live luxurious lives with our children.

I must confess that, as with any new relationship, the beginning is key. There is bound to be some measure of weariness. Some of you take this as the person's dislike of you or vice versa. Like every relationship, you work on getting to know the people you will call mom and dad, brother or sister. Your spouse will do the same with your family. By the time you become successful at this, the weariness and suspicion will melt away on its own. I agree that some cases may differ where family members can never be satisfied no matter what you do; however, note that this is not the norm. Love and respect beget love and respect, especially with the backing of the Lord God.

Sometimes, behaviour such as the words or actions of extended family members can hurt much more than they were intended to and can take a toll on a couple's relationship. What you should not entertain is if this behaviour is a direct attempt aimed at breaking your marriage apart. Be mindful if the individuals are abusing drugs or alcohol, as they often cause conflict within the family and exhibit a lack of respect toward you and your spouse. If any of these are impacting your marriage negatively, you need to take steps to protect your marriage, like seeking professional help from your pastor or Christian counsellor.

It would be very presumptuous to think that everyone has the most loving and understanding in-laws or extended family. Most issues resulting from family members and in-laws can be resolved easily by setting some boundaries and having a respectful talk with those concerned and explaining exactly why you find the behaviour disconcerting and unacceptable. It is the case that most of you find it easier to complain and vent to someone else to temporarily relieve your stress. However, this is not going to help nor is it likely to change the situation. It might end up causing more problems for all involved.

Complaining about an in-law's behaviour to your spouse is also not advisable as this will only lead to conflicts between you and your spouse. My friend Trish had a fallout with her husband's family and whenever she complained to her husband, he told her angrily to fix it and stormed away. He felt like he was being put in the middle and did not want his family to think he was henpecked. After seeking the Lord's help, Trish finally summoned up the courage to have "that dreaded talk" with them. She discussed her concerns about the impact of their unhelpful attitude and disrespectful behaviour toward her, and her father-in-law saw reason with her and apologized for their inconsiderate action.

An extended family can either support the marriage, be uncaring and neutral, or add stress to the relationship. Note here that if your agenda is to change their behaviour, you will be setting yourself up for failure. This is because you cannot change anyone; change must come from you and you cannot control anyone's behaviours either. You can only control how you respond and react toward them. It is possible to have a happy and healthy marriage, even if you have difficult parents or in-laws. Please forget the hype about the wicked family or in-laws. If you are struggling with the pressure from family, try building some hedges that can help you successfully form a new family while reducing or doing away with conflict brought about by pressure from the extended family. Husbands, some of you are so self-centred and selfish that you think your family of origin is the only important one in this relationship!

My suggestion would be that you must first decide what you want to do, and then put it into action. It can be as simple as agreeing with your spouse on your set of values as a couple. How do you want extended family members to be treated? It does not matter whose parents or family; the same treatment must be given to all and be consistent while communicating with the extended family. A united front is a plus in any conversation with extended family. Be aware that you must not contradict one another as extended family members will notice this discrepancy and inconsistency and will immediately take advantage of them. It is often the case that spouses discuss everything but financial help for extended family.

Make sure that you discuss your expectations regarding how to handle matters relating to how you intend to provide financial help to relatives without letting them ruin your home. I have a friend whose husband always sends financial help to his family and every other person who is "in need" but comfortably forgets that she has family who expects some form of help from her too. She feels bad about this, but reasons that since he does this for others, it should come as natural for him too to do for her family. Whenever this happens, she feels let down and says nothing. She makes excuses to her family. They understand that if it were up to her, she would never fail to give to them. She finds it difficult to point this behaviour out to her husband. She feels angry and resentful toward him and remains sad and bitter about it but says nothing to him. After all, he has a brain! This most often impedes her. You can see here that there is a communication breakdown. Speak up and "do not give the devil a foothold" (Ephesians 4:27). Not talking to each other is an invitation to the devil! It is an opportunity Satan will not let go of as it is a tool he uses quite effectively against couples. He does not need a second invitation—it is one of the major factors that lead to marital breakdown.

Ever wondered why Ruth said "your people, my people" in the following verse?

> But Ruth replied, "Don't urge me to leave you or to turn back from you.
>
> Where you go, I will go, and where you stay, I will stay. Your people will be my people and your God my God. Where you die, I will die, and there

I will be buried. May the LORD deal
with me, be it ever so severely, if
even death separates you and me."
(Ruth 1:16–17)

How true is this in marriage? There could never
have been a better example of steadfast love than that
displayed by Naomi toward Ruth in this passage. We
must view our spouse's parents as our own. Nothing
stopped Naomi from just jumping ship and leaving
Ruth all alone! But she knew better! There are times
when we have been hurt by our in-laws; it must be
noted that keeping a score of the many ills dealt to us
would only serve as a block or bridge in our lives as
couples. They might not want to accept you as part
of the family, but you can eventually win them over
by your faith and trust in Christ.

Holding on to past hurts not only infringes upon
the husband and wife's relationship but on the family
functioning as well. The concept of an eye for an
eye should not apply here. When we vow to love
and to hold, a lot more goes into this than we think.
In simple terms, it is through thick or thin, high or
low waters, mountains or valleys, good in-laws or
bad ones. A teenage girl once said to me, "Before I
get married, I would give my fiancé a questionnaire
containing all the information about him that might
slip my knowledge when we get married!" He has to
be privy to everything I can tolerate!

Sadly enough, I do not think that there is any questionnaire that could be exhaustive and adequate to cover all that might happen in marriage. It must always be remembered that couples are two different people whom God in His wisdom has united. True oneness can only be achieved if a couple starts bearing each other's burdens in the truest sense. The belief that only the dominant party's desires matter here should not be so. Each spouse has feelings, and as a result, needs and desires differ too. Couples must agree on how in-laws will be treated from the very beginning of the marriage as this goes a long way to eliminating the conflict that might eventually arise because one spouse feels that her own people are neglected or come second in the order of things. If this is not done from the onset, couples will find themselves harbouring unexplained bitterness against one another.

Father, mother, sister, brother, and of course, the extended family—it does not matter who. Just prepare for the journey and open yourself up for the thrill and adventure. Hey, it is a journey of a lifetime and we have neither detours nor quick exits here. You might as well be ready to go all the way and enjoy it as much as you can.

"In your anger do not sin. Do not let the sun go down while you are still angry."

—Ephesians 4:26

Chapter Twelve

Disagreements

Marriage is between two entirely different individuals with completely different upbringings, values, and orientation. To put it plainly, there are basically little or no similarities between them. Even if they were raised in the same home, they would have a different outlook on things because that is what makes each individual unique and special. Because of this, there are bound to be disagreements, and these are the ones that can make your marriages stronger and richer. When you resolve to appreciate each other's differences or uniqueness and not try to change them, you begin to see marriage as God intended it—a partnership that was meant to last till death do you part. In this, you are meant to come together as a team and combine your strengths and support each other's weaknesses, making a conscious effort not to dwell too much on your partner's negative qualities. When this happens, you get to know each other better and, in the process, know your own capabilities. Learn to use these to deepen your connection with your spouse.

Disagreements happen in marriages; in fact, there are no marriages that do not have them! God made each one of us different to add diversity to lives. He knew man and wife would disagree, but there is a stipulation in Ephesians 4:26 **stating**, "In your anger do not sin." Do not let the sun go down while you are still angry. Because you are two different beings raised and brought up in different ways, you have different ideologies and mentalities. Note here disagreeing is not considered a sin. It is not unique to you alone; every couple will at some point disagree with each other. It only becomes a sin when you allow it to fester, resulting in resentment, thus giving the devil a foothold to tempt you to sin.

Forget the make-believe scenes from movies and your favourite romance novels for a while. Disagreements are real; it is how you handle them that matters. The Lord God knew this was the best thing to happen: can you imagine being married to a "yes" man or woman? Or maybe your clone? Somebody who has all your good and bad habits who does everything you do! There would be nothing that would come as a surprise to you again because you would both react to situations the same way. What a bore that would be! I am sure that even in this case, there would still be some measure of resentment because we are human and can never be pleased.

God never meant it to be like that. That is why He created Eve, who was so different from Adam, even though she came from a part of him. This shows us that God meant man and wife to enjoy the journey of self-discovery, intimacy, and live their lives to the fullest. He knew that in making them different, sparks were bound to fly, and if resolved in the right way would lead to a very rich, fulfilling, and enduring partnership. You are to celebrate this difference and build a companionship where gradually you start putting the other person first without even a second's thought, and you live for the good of each other. Because if one wins, the other does too! Do not wait for the other partner or spouse to make a mistake so that you can bring up the past disagreement and show him how hurt one can be! Be careful not to attack each other. Blaming and shaming each other can never help you build a strong, fulfilling, and fruitful marital bond. Realize that you are on the same team where there is neither a winner nor a loser. To get to this stage is not an overnight occurrence! It requires a Christ-centred mindset as you take baby steps daily and love wholeheartedly, a love which Jesus Christ has exhibited for us to emulate.

For this to become practicable in your lives, or for you to get to this stage, you must first learn to love in the truest sense! Learn to pick your battles. When you disagree, do not fight cheaply because once words are said, they cannot be retrieved nor taken back no matter how much you apologize! The Bible states in

Proverbs 10:20–21 that "The tongue of the righteous is a choice silver but the heart of the wicked is of little value. The lips of the righteous nourish many but fools die for lack of sense."

Well, it is accurate that a righteous tongue nourishes but the fool dies for lack of sense. It is often the case that we get carried away by our emotions and spew out all the rubbish we have had buried deep inside waiting for just an opportunity like this to allow our pent-up anger and bitterness to well up! We say everything without reserve. As the Bible states, how can we curse with the same mouth we use to praise God?

Hold it for a second! I know we get angry, but as I stated earlier, the same Bible enjoins us to be angry but sin not. Well, you can say "I am only human and do not forget he/she said some bad words too!" Okay, but can two wrongs make a right? How do you justify this outburst? God has given us power over our tongues, and if you submit yourself entirely to Him even in times like these, He helps you through and you can still have this argument without pulling the other person down. It is always the case that you can then turn what would have been destructive into a healthy display of dissatisfaction, or an avenue for making your grievances known without resorting to jungle tactics or the mean girl's punch.

You must learn to walk in each other's shoes. Only then will you realize that what hurts you has the same ability or potential to hurt the other person too.

Look at it as the case of "your shoes, my shoes." Clear communication of your feelings and expectations with your spouse is an essential key to a happy, healthy, and lifelong committed marriage. Listen to your spouse without interrupting, especially when she/he is trying to tell you how she feels. Resist the urge to shut her out, criticize, or jump to conclusions. This is not the time to give her the advice you have been looking for, a way of offering for some time.

It is, therefore, worthwhile to take a moment and ask yourself this question: How do I communicate? In 1 Corinthians 13:1–3, it says:

> If I speak in the tongues of men or of angels, but do not have love, I am only a resounding gong or a clanging cymbal. If I have the gift of prophecy and can fathom all mysteries and all knowledge, and if I have a faith that can move mountains, but do not have love, I am nothing. If I give all I possess to the poor and give over my body to hardship that I may boast, but do not have love, I gain nothing.

To my understanding, true love would never take undue advantage of the other person. It would not violate another person's body just for his own selfish pleasure. True love is giving; it gives even when it hurts to do so. It puts others first and works to help the loved one to grow while always forgiving and encouraging them. Love never wants the loved one broken nor distraught. Neither would it encourage another person to disobey God's law, instead it nurtures and builds up. You must have found yourself wondering several times why whenever you try to carry out a civil conversation with your spouse, you both end up quarrelling, to the extent that now you have both decided to be civil and just avoid any controversial topics. How then do you expect to grow and love each other truly and be blessed in the process?

Marriage is not a boxing match, as I have stated. When you decide to see it as a dance, where two of you move in sync, with one leading while the other follows, you will begin to understand the need for both of you to be in the relationship. If there is no coordination, then you will not be successful as you will keep tripping over each other. The long-standing love that will see you through marriage is a choice, which means it is intentional and purposeful. You resolve to love no matter what! This is love where you can see the shortcomings in your spouse and instead of taking the exit, you sit still and resolve to love him/her and work things out anyway.

Unresolved conflict and anger push your spouse into a corner where they feel helpless and unwanted. It raises walls and barriers that were never there in your relationship and breeds deep-rooted anger, resentment, and frustrations. It is the destroyer of your peace and happiness. Sometimes it is so deeply entrenched that doubts about the validity of you and your marriage begin to gnaw away at you, making you wish you had not gotten into this relationship in the first place. Some of you immediately try to fix this "mistake" by opting for the quickest and easiest way out: divorce! Others decide to compromise and stay, thus bidding goodbye to their happiness and satisfaction because of the unresolved issues. The brave and determined resolve to solve this problem and find their lost peace and happiness.

Bear in mind that not all disagreements are necessarily geared toward the dissolution of your marriage. Remember, I mentioned that because you are different entities, you are bound to disagree on certain issues. You disagree because you are not the same. You do not have the same likes. Your spouse might love a colour that you thoroughly abhor, or a sport you cannot even understand in its essence. That is all right. However, if you find yourself in a situation like this, do not make the mistake of trying to change how he or she feels about that thing or person.

I remember quite early in my marriage, my husband had a friend I just could not stand because I saw him as a big liar and of very poor character. I got infuriated every time he came over as I tried to be at my best and not show him exactly how I felt about him. The best way out for me was to have a civil discussion about how I felt with my husband. He understood my point and we did not have to argue about this again. He believed I was welcome to my opinion and tried his best not to encourage frequent visits from him. My point here is that, instead of this causing a rift in our relationship, we grew closer and I felt loved because he had understood my point of view. No matter how many frustrations you might have, you should not try blackmailing or manipulating your spouse into changing how he or she feels as there is nothing to be gained from this. Just be truthful about your feelings.

If my husband had not listened to my words and heard my reasons but tried forcing or manipulating me into changing how I felt about his friend, I would have stuck to my guns and made a fuss whenever he came around, and this would have eventually caused a lot of problems in our marriage. As partners, you must always try to listen respectfully to each other in a way that makes the other person feel heard, loved, valued, and respected. If you do not listen to your spouse's ideas, and ask questions for clarification, refraining from the "I know it all" attitude, how will you understand and communicate that you love her and have her back?

Some couples love the concept of just winning an argument. They do not have the patience to understand what the argument is all about. They neither have the time to see past their egos nor to unearth the real reason for their spouse's displeasure. The typical reaction is to go for the kill and just put the other person down. It is not only necessary but mandatory for spouses to possess the skill of active and attentive listening because this facilitates the free flow of communication. It also results in greater love and understanding in the marriage, leading to fulfillment and reduced misunderstandings.

When I was growing up, my dad had inspirational paintings on the wall. The one that intrigued me most went like this: "The family that prays together stays together." I mulled over this painting whenever I walked past, and in my innocent mind, I felt bad when for one reason or another, we could not pray as often as we needed to. I felt that we were not going to stay together as the painting claimed. What is the point I am trying to make here? The power of prayer can never be underestimated nor overemphasized, especially as a couple. It will not hurt you if you turn to God before discussing something with your spouse. God will take control of the conversation and instead of words of pride, aggression, and hate coming out of your mouths, you will speak blessings and peace upon each another.

The Bible says in Ephesians 6:12, "For our struggle is not against flesh and blood, but against the rulers, against the authorities, against the powers of this dark world and against the spiritual forces of evil in the heavenly realms." Our only weapon against the enemy is our prayer. We must never cease to pray as a couple or as individuals together and for one another. Most often, the devil uses these tricks in the form of arguments to throw us off our path to fulfillment and unity in marriage. Our attack should not be resignation but to submit ourselves and commit these issues to the Lord God by asking for His wisdom and protection. We must be careful concerning this matter; the devil will never give up. He will continue to look for an avenue to take advantage of.

No matter how good you have become as friends, keeping count of all wrongs builds a wedge between a husband and wife, and as spouses, you can never fully embrace the essence of marriage. Some of you hold unto hurts and refuse to forgive because it serves or fuels a purpose. How else are you going to be able to bring it up if you dared to forget it? You even want it carved in stone, so you always remember! Abuses and curses lead to disrespect and apathy. Hello! If we are all made in God's image, what then is our purpose in marriage? Everyone has a purpose in marriage. We must learn to live for each other and be present, rejoice, and praise God for all His goodness. Be transparent with each other and be fulfilled in your roles as partners. A wedding ring is a visible reminder of an inward commitment you made to your spouse before God and man. It is a symbol for those who care to look, and a constant reminder of the promise you made each other in front of God to love and to hold, to cherish till death do you part. This promise must not be taken casually; it is to be protected with all you have. It is not a promise that is supposed to last until you fall out of love and are ready to move on to the next presentable option that shows up in the guise of, *I do not love you anymore!* The Lord God had His reasons for making this bond a lifelong one.

And husbands/wives, if you all share some attributes of God, then whom are you cursing? The Creator or the creation? Does God leave any exit clause for you when you are tempted to ask when you can throw in the towel? The answer here is *never!* You are to stay married to each other through sickness and pain, till death do you part. Marriage comes with a lifetime warranty, and I think this is very wonderful on God's part to grant us this service. When we buy a product, it comes with a warranty from the manufacturer, and we are to return it for service if it has defects or get an exchange or a refund. So, who best to handle our problems than the Creator and author of marriage? Parents are the foundation around which children build their lives. This foundation must be strong, so that as they look back at their lives as children; they resolve to do better or as well as their parents did.

Mistakes or Choices?

When you decide to marry, it is a conscious choice. You already have in mind what type of home and life you want. And believe me, if you want a happy home, you will get it because you are ready to put in all you have to make it so. You are determined and have resolved to make a difference. You must take the appropriate steps and measures to bring your dreams to the fore. You must understand that happiness cannot be gotten by peeping into the neighbours' yard to see how they are doing it. Neither can you be happy by always creeping on your friends' social media pages to see what is new in their lives. Rather, it comes from wanting it, from deep within you where you least expected, and floods into your whole being, saturating and touching everyone you meet.

The only thing needed here is that you be you and present in every way. Be honest and truthful, and God will help make everything come to pass. Proverbs 4:23 **says**, "Above all else, guard your heart, for everything you do flows from it." Why do you need to do this? Because your adversary, the devil, is not sleeping, and he will try his best to derail you from your goal. He wants you to quit before you even start! So, he will bring about distractions in your lives that make you feel less than worthy. I have often heard people say, "I always get what I want." Well, so true, because they have resolved to get it and have put in the effort needed, the machinery in place to spin them through all hurdles and get to where they want to be. Every successful person has this inborn determination and drive to speak these things into being by their actions. Stop expecting disappointment as your expectations will come to pass. Like I mentioned earlier, be positive and know that the Lord is with you. He will never leave you.

You must not forget that God punishes every act of unfaithfulness. It is not practicable for you to just wake up one morning and decide that you have suddenly fallen out of love and you need to move on or suddenly realized that you have made a huge mistake and your spouse is not what you need after all. It is very sad to hear couples exchange all insults and profanities because they have decided to break ties with their spouse. The question I always ask is, was there anything you ever loved or admired about this person? Why the sudden barrage of insults? Some go to the extent of calling each other the worst kinds of names. Well, grow up! It takes two to tango, and I would like to mention here that our God does not sleep, no matter how heartless your spouse gets during your marriage. If you resolve to be hardworking and put things in order, the Lord will surely help you. Always bear in mind that change starts with you!

Divorce is a sign that you have given up on God, your dreams, and that you have no courage to go on. You have lost all faith in God, who made marriage possible. It is a sign that you have failed yourself. It is not God who has failed you! I would like to remind you that the Bible says God does not allow us to be tempted beyond what we can bear. He will surely make a way out for you if you can only trust in Him.

But I want you to know that the son of
man has authority on earth to forgive
sins.

—Matthew 9:6

Chapter Thirteen

Forgiveness

I have often heard statements like "I will never forgive him for what he has done to me!" It is common knowledge that you get so infuriated with your spouse that such words come easily! Arguably, you have been terribly wronged! Vowing not to forgive? Now that is a whole new story. Ever wondered what would become of you, your spouse, and your relationship if you were to follow through with this? You set yourself up for failure not only spiritually but emotionally and physically. Your health begins to deteriorate. Forgiveness is most often the most difficult thing to do as your ego always comes into play and you strive to exercise your rights to fair understanding and being heard. Let us take a moment and see what forgiveness really means! According to the Bible, there are situations where you find yourself wondering why you must forgive when you have been offended. Your spouse knew what he was doing

215

and did not pay you a second thought, so why should you forgive such behaviour? Sometimes you are so hurt that you do not want to think of the possibility of reconciliation, let alone forgiveness.

Unforgiveness is just struggling to hold on to something we need to let go of. When walking in unforgiveness, we fail to realize that there is such freedom in being able to forgive instead of wallowing in guilt and resentment. We fail to forgive because we are first looking forward to the person changing or apologizing. This does not end here as we fail to pay ourselves this courtesy, because even when we need to forgive ourselves, it seems easiest to wait until we've grown and moved past what we've done to a point where we no longer remember or it ceases to hurt us. However, a closer look at the life of Jesus shows us another way.

Although we have been steeped in sin and pain, He did not hold this against us. Instead, He chose to forgive us, overlooking all our shortcomings. What would have happened to us if He had waited for just that moment that we would change or grow before forgiving? He loved us where we were at and paid the price for all of our sins, past and future, holding back nothing.

The best part of it is that He didn't just die for just a fraction of humanity, but for everyone—irrespective of race, creed, or colour, the good, the bad, the broken, the hurtful person or the poor. He loves you where you are at right now and wants to have a relationship with you. When we come to the realization of the sacrifice and huge debt Christ paid on our behalf, we then can gain an understanding of what God did for us. This is the easiest and best way to learn about forgiveness and what it takes to forgive. It is common knowledge that the Bible is full of messages about forgiveness, but when it comes down to it, few people can identify exactly what the Bible actually says about it.

A look at the Bible shows that forgiveness is not a new concept. The most conspicuous example is Joseph's forgiveness of his brothers who had sold him into slavery. Although wronged by his siblings, Joseph decided to forgive as he states in Genesis 50:20: "You intended to harm me, but God intended it for good to accomplish what is now being done, the saving of many lives."

Forgiveness is for our benefit because the weight of unforgiveness always feels like a huge burden we are carrying around and refusing to let go. I am a very good example of this. A few months ago, someone I had done everything within my power to help hurt me so badly that whenever I drove past the turnoff to her house, I felt a surge of rage welling up inside me, and I felt a constriction in my chest. Whenever this feeling came up, I would immediately feel the need for vengeance. I wanted her to know how much she had hurt me. I would not be able to think of anything else until I got back home. I talked about it to anyone who would listen; this did not help as I was both the jury and the judge! I had told my story so many times that I could easily have told it in my sleep!

Finally, like a light turned on in my brain one day, I was driving past this street again and the same feelings welled up, and I just whispered a silent prayer, and at that very moment, I felt a peace like never before. It was like a heavy weight had been lifted off my shoulders. Weeks and months passed; I never thought about her again. After a long while, this person's name came up in conversation, and I suddenly realized that I had neither spoken nor thought about her for months, even though I had constantly driven down her street. I mentioned this to my husband, and I decided to follow it up by driving down her street to gauge my reaction!

To my greatest surprise, I felt so calm just passing by her house to the extent that I felt like seeing or checking to see how she was doing! This was a great shock, especially as I never believed I was ever going to forgive her. It dawned on me then that I had just been carrying an unnecessary burden around and feeling like a victim!

You are too precious and cannot afford to give anyone the right to make you feel that way in your life. Above all, let it stand between you and God, as mentioned earlier on. You have a choice to make, and only you can make it. Imagine taking poison and hoping it kills your enemy instead of you! Well, let's face it, no one but you would die if you tried that. I would like to add here that all through this period of unforgiveness, I felt as if God was nowhere near me! It was like I was on barren land. The transformation I realized took place the day I decided to let God handle all my pain. It led me to be closer to God. I became and felt very free and light. No longer was that pain holding me down. I was no longer stuck in my past and afraid of moving forward.

I am thankful to God for setting me free because I would have wasted many years struggling with bitterness and resentment instead of moving forward and living my life in joy and happiness. Since forgiving, I have grown both spiritually and emotionally as I am no longer wasting my precious time thinking and talking about someone else and feeling hurt and let down in the process. I now know that unforgiveness hurts only me as the other person might not even be aware of the hurt they have caused me. I wished I had let go faster than I did, then all the hurt and pain I went through would never have happened.

Let me mention that forgiveness does not mean forgetting, and I have checked and there is no mention of this in the Bible. Sometimes the hurts are such that they are not easily forgotten. But when we decide to submit to the Lord and let Him heal our hurts, it becomes possible to forgive and also forget. The only thing forgiveness does is helps you come to terms with what has occurred and removes the hard and bitter feelings linked to it. If you are thinking of breaking a relationship because the other person hurt you terribly in the worst possible way, even if you do not want to continue with the relationship, you should make some effort to forgive them for what they have done. If you find it difficult to do, just leave it to the Lord and He will help you through the hard times, pain, and bitterness, and also give you the ability to overcome troubles.

Great healing always comes in the wake of forgiveness because when I held onto the hurts, I always felt heavy and sick, but upon forgiving, I found new strength and physical wellness and well-being because God had also forgiven me. Matthew 9:6 says, "But I want you to know that the son of man has authority on earth to forgive sins." So, he said to the paralyzed man, "Get up, take your mat and go home." We must understand that we do not have to work hard for forgiveness as it is a gift from God and must be freely given as many times as the need arises. Matthew 18:21–22, in the parable of the unmerciful servant, says, "Then Peter came to Jesus and asked, 'Lord, how many times shall I forgive my brother or sister who sins against me? Up to seven times?' Jesus answered, 'I tell you, not seven times, but seventy-seven times.'"

The Bible also states in 2 Corinthians 12:9: "But he said to me, 'My grace is sufficient for you, for my power is made perfect in weakness.'" Therefore, I will boast all the more gladly about my weaknesses, so that Christ's power may rest on me. Do not ever forget that prayer is a balm for every affliction. It is a remedy for every infirmity, and whether you are afflicted with thorns in the flesh or fighting to overcome unforgiveness, you should give yourself to prayer. Never despair if an answer has not been given to the first prayer. Persevere and pray without ceasing, just continue praying. Most times God allows troubles our way just to teach us to pray and depend solely on the Lord. So, whenever troubles come your way, rise up and pray!

I would like to say here that just as mentioned earlier, whenever two people from different backgrounds or parts of the world decide to take the plunge and get married, there are bound to be arguments. These are not meant to break you up but to make you better people. It is not how many times you argue but what efforts you put into making up that matter. I learned a very important lesson while growing up: That it is the bigger person who forgives, as I was so often admonished to forgive. I must confess here that this was a very difficult thing for me to practice, and every time I tried forgiving, I felt as if I was swallowing a very bitter pill. This was because I was steeped in self-righteousness and felt I could never be accused of any wrongdoing.

I cannot begin to tell you how many times I silently resolved in the face of conflict never to be the first to apologize. I felt I was always being taken undue advantage of because of my forgiving nature. There was always a valid reason why I did not have to make the first move. I can't begin to say how many times I allowed the conflict to linger in the face of this argument. It was always the other person's fault, and I felt they should know better, realize their mistakes, and then seek forgiveness. I guess in my own little world, I always felt that I was right; after all, nobody wants to be taken for granted. Why should I always be the first to forgive? You must agree, this argument is very correct and valid!

Well, are there any reasons for us to forgive? A closer look at the Bible tells us that unforgiveness in any relationship can act as a wedge that stands between God and us. The Bible further states that we have all sinned and have fallen short of the glory of God. Through the grace of God, we have been forgiven and set free from our sin and guilt. If at this very moment, we were asked to take stock of our lives, could we sincerely say we have not done anything awful to God or man? So, if God can forgive us of all the wickedness, we should be ready to forgive others as often as the need arises. Matthew 6:14–15 states that "if you forgive other people when they sin against you, your heavenly Father will also forgive you. But if you do not forgive others their sins, your Father will not forgive your sins."

We can see a very close relationship between our decision to forgive and the father's wish. He does not want to hold us to our sins; rather, we tie his hands when we choose not to forgive others. We can then invariably say that forgiveness is for our benefit because walking in unforgiveness blocks our interaction with God, and we walk around carrying a heavy burden, feeling like a victim when the Lord wants to relieve us and set us free. How many of us really practise real forgiveness? Forgiveness is often one of the hardest things to do, and it's not only in marriages but also in any relationship that we are involved in that we need to learn true forgiveness.

I would like to say that there is no injunction in the Bible for us to forget, but we are asked expressly to forgive so our father in heaven will forgive us too. When we purposely choose to forgive a wrong done to us, even when we remember it, it can no longer hurt us. I know it is quite difficult to decide to forgive but remember that the Lord knows it all; just cast whatever is troubling you upon Him and He will take care of the rest. With time, you will be able to remember it without any bitterness or anger.

"Till death do us part." What an amazing promise for a couple to make to each other! It's an abiding, true, and all-encompassing one! The Bible tells us to let our yes be yes and our no be no! This promise made at the altar between man, woman, and God in front of an audience that has been specially handpicked to witness this amazing union and encourage the new couple in their new life is great. You now realize that your spouse is the most amazing gift from God that you are meant to cherish and treasure. When you hurt one another, choose to forgive and work things out instead of throwing in the towel and opting out of the marriage. It is much easier to break relationships than to mend them. Work on your marriage and stay together.

Growing up often happens when our children arrive on the scene. We are suddenly faced with the realization that we are responsible for another life, and this brings us to a sudden awakening. I remember how much in awe I was when I had my first child. I could not believe what came over me. I would call it a surge of affection that I never knew I was capable of. I knew instantly that I owed it to my daughter to be the best I could ever be. I wanted to give her the world but not without Christ. I recognized that I was just a custodian and I was answerable to God if anything went wrong. I determined then that every milestone was going to be committed to God. This bore great results, and when I look back at my life, I understand that I would never have been able to do this without the guidance of my heavenly Father.

When it begins to make sense, we realize that everyone gets a wife or husband, but those who sacrifice themselves for their husband or wife are just God's blessing to the union. I am not talking about you taking your life to please your husband or wife! What I am saying is that as a couple, we must step away from the "me mentality" and become the men or women God has called us to be. A quick look at the woman in Proverbs 31:10–20 casts some light on this:

> A wife of noble character who can find? She is worth far more than rubies.

Her husband has full confidence in her and lacks nothing of value. She brings him good, not harm, all the days of her life. She selects wool and flax and works with eager hands. She is like the merchant ships, bringing her food from afar. She gets up while it is still night; she provides food for her family and portions for her female servants. She considers a field and buys it; out of her earnings she plants a vineyard. She sets about her work vigorously; her arms are strong for her tasks. She sees that her trading is profitable, and her lamp does not go out at night. In her hand, she holds the distaff and grasps the spindle with her fingers. She opens her arms to the poor and extends her hand to the needy.

Make no mistake here. The Bible does not mention anywhere that this woman was perfect. It says instead that this woman did not need anyone telling her, her worth, as she knew she was precious and worthwhile and loved. As women, God has bestowed upon us great potential and given us the privilege of bringing forth life and giving birth to our children. He sees us as capable and as a result, we must fulfill the call of God on us to be virtuous and capable. This woman was not selfish but very selfless, faithful, and did not only enrich her life but also that of those around her like her female servants. How many of us women feel that those working for us are deserving of anything but the scraps? Our lives are such that we surround ourselves with much while watching others working for us or around us wallow in penury. For us to emulate the Proverbs 31 woman, we are not to become superwomen but just to fulfill our daily obligations wholeheartedly, whether it be in being good to our husbands or family members. We must love and cherish each relationship we find ourselves in and be truthful to earn the trust of others. She channelled her energies toward making life good for all instead of spending her time checking or creeping up on others to see what they were up to.

She was the reason her husband was respected in the courts! She tended not only to her household but to everyone around her. She mastered the art of putting the pieces of her life and marriage together. She had a strength of character and playing the act of the helpless damsel in distress was not in her books. She was a woman of great intelligence, even though there was no mention of accolades or degrees or qualifications against her name. She was the daughter of Zion in the truest sense of the word, for her validation did not come from man but from her Creator, God!

She had the ability to impact and change things for the better. Her world revolved around pleasing her God and enriching the lives of others! She was very faithful and worked on preparing her heart for those things that could help bring her closer to God, by practising daily, no matter what she was engaged in or where she was in her walk with God or in life. As we go through life, we must realize that to be this kind of woman, we must be truthful and earn others' trust. Always bear in mind that you have been bestowed with a lot of attributes to be used to enrich not only your life, but the people around you as well. This woman was full of contentment. She understood that no good marriage comes wrapped in a parcel—you must work on it. You are a vital part of the family— appreciate, love, and respect yourself.

The most notable roles of a woman are daughter, sister, mother, friend, wife, and so on. A woman can adapt to any role she finds herself in. As a couple, you must be committed to each other while fulfilling these roles. Invest in your marriage. This cannot be overemphasized. It is not the duty nor responsibility of only one of you to fulfill, but a joint effort that bears long-lasting fruit. In this journey, there is no room for one partner to be a know-it-all and condescending. Be respectful of each other's feelings. We might think that we are great at hiding the way we feel. I would, however, like to state here that we normally fail woefully at this as the other partner feels undermined or most often taken for granted. The best advice I can proffer here is that we should act according to the dictates of the Bible, where we are enjoined to be angry but sin not, and we should not let the sun go down on our anger. Holding out on your spouse amounts to this. Let it out and be prepared to talk and work it out. Have a verbal workout with your spouse, not a war of words. Note that a workout is geared toward and targets parts of the body that need to be toned, shaped, or recontoured, and the results are always pleasant, whereas a war only leaves devastation, regrets, and brokenness behind. Unresolved conflict and anger push our spouse into a corner where they feel helpless and unwanted. It raises walls that were never there in our relationship.

Transparency

Have you ever wondered why God created Adam and Eve naked and not ashamed of this fact? We all know that God is all-knowing, and He does not work in confusion, so there must have been a reason for this. I am sure that he intended for husband and wife to be completely open, exposed, vulnerable, and available to one another. No reservations were imposed upon these two. Total and absolute transparency existed between them as they were discovering what it meant to have a spouse. They revelled in each other and no mental, physical, or spiritual walls existed between them as they could communicate with God whenever they so desired.

This is the opposite of what is happening in our marriage! We have new gadgets with which we have to do photo authentication for access to be granted to us, or we do a thumb imprint. Most of us are just delighted at this because it means our spouse will not be able to infringe upon our private rendezvous that we carry on with the help of these instruments. I remember prior to this period of technological freedom, people complained bitterly about how their spouse went through their phone and found "private material" not meant for their eyes! What a relief this must have brought! I am not trying to condone spouses checking our phones in our absence here. However, if there exists transparency between you, would the need to do this arise? What would you need to hide from your spouse?

It is often the case that due to a lot of factors, the importance of being or having transparency in a relationship is often downplayed, scoffed at, and mocked. We find it very normal if our spouse cannot access our phones nor emails. Our passwords are changed frequently to prevent this from ever happening. If there is an indication of a breach, we treat it like the person has committed an unpardonable crime.

Why are we hiding stuff from the one person we claim to love above all else? We only hide things if we are guilty of a sin, some inappropriate behaviour, or something that we know would not be easily condoned by our spouse. We are aware that if found out, it could cause major chaos and breakdown in our home or relationship. So why do we engage in such disparaging behaviour that sets us up for failure? For any marriage or relationship to succeed, there must be complete transparency between both partners? If there is one place that has no place or zero tolerance for secrecy, it is marriage. For a strong marriage, both spouses must determine to be completely transparent with each other. When I say completely transparent, I do not mean hiding some things and only talking about other less important ones.

It was not a mistake that God made woman and man partners; God created you for one person to share love and life with, to be completely vulnerable physically, emotionally, mentally, and spiritually. This is one person you can truly be yourself with! Being transparent with each other removes the unwanted barriers, prevents secrecy, promotes longevity, and improves intimacy in your marriage. For complete transparency to be implemented in marriage, spouses must determine to be as open as possible with one another. Transparency must be held in high priority between the spouses and even among the children. I remember a very well-meaning friend confronted me about the mistake I had made in not being able to just give her an advance without my husband's knowledge. She felt, as a woman, we had to hide some truths from our spouses. I must say she was not very impressed when I told her this was impossible for me to do as I shared everything with my husband.

I am not trying to say some things can be transparent while others are anathema. Spouses must be open with each other as this prevents resentment and any disgruntled feelings from cropping up in the relationship. The number one killer of relationships is one spouse's over-controlling behaviour when it comes to finances along with a lukewarm and passive attitude toward other aspects of family life. This is often the case with the husbands.

No one can fix you. The potential is within you. Neither can you try to fix another as any change must first come from you. When you have decided to enter the relationship, just determine and align yourself for success.

As iron sharpens iron,
so one person sharpens another.

—Proverbs 27:17

Chapter Fourteen

Godly Living

Friends

When I wake up each morning, it occurs to me that it is a brand-new day and I must allow the Lord to work in me so that I can be the best I can ever be. I turn my marriage over to him because at no point do I try to claim that I have everything under control and that the devil has stopped fighting against this institution. Like a child learning to walk, I still need my Creator's hand in all that concerns me every step of the way. If you want a marriage that is amazing, fulfilling, and has the Lord's stamp of approval on it, then commit it to Him and He will see you through.

Friends come in different forms, sizes, and shapes, with none of them ever being the same. It is often the case that it is said that birds of the same feather flock together. This is true as most friends may share similar traits, but no two friends bring or impact your life in the same way. Some friends become more like family, and it is always a joy to be in their company, while no matter what you try or do, others always remain more like acquaintances. I have had some friends who have been so conniving, needy, greedy, and manipulating, and time spent with these types of people drains you and makes you feel hollow, while some other friends are so caring, understanding, undemanding, and very generous.

It was not long before I realized that spending too much time with friends who are not common friends between spouses leads to a lot of trouble. They only create discontent in the other spouse as they portray everything as marvellous to make one feel inadequate for marrying someone outside that circle or not good enough. The picture or impression they present is that of bliss in their own marriage and home, while yours sucks! Understand that the people you spend most of your time with often hold the most influence in your life. I am not trying to dispute the value or importance of having friends; I know some contribute an important part to your personal development and growth, and this is very great. However, do not forget that some possess too much wisdom you can do without as they can usually offer too many voices and opinions. Pause for a while here and consider what happens when you go to them after a fight or disagreement with your spouse over some issue. I am sure as you are reading this, you are beginning to have a picture of what I am saying here. Most of you feel it is just natural for you to go to friends for advice in cases like this! You are supposed to be protecting your wives and women; you are to be your husband's helper or helpmeet. How are you fulfilling these roles if you run to friends to wash your dirty linen with them in public? When you come back from such meetings, does their counsel sincerely help you solve the issues with your spouse? It does not, because too many friends and too many voices can be dangerous for your marriage.

While there are potential dangers of friendships outside your marriage, there are also benefits of having close friends! I am by no means discounting the importance of friends in your life but have friends who sow the positive things into your life. Couples should have common friends: friends who have or share the same interests.

Most of you enjoy spending time with friends while leaving your spouse at home. This to an extent is healthy as you do not *always* have to be with your spouse, and you should be able to spend time away! It is true that most of you prefer spending time with your friends. This begins to take precedence over time spent with your spouse as it makes it impossible for you to be with the one you vowed to spend your whole life with.

Suddenly, a lot begins to change about you as you imbibe new habits that no longer include or involve your spouse. Sometimes, if this is not checked in time, you lose touch with your real self as you gradually become like one or more of your friends. When this happens, you may feel yourself drifting away from your spouse and finding that he or she is not the same person you married. She fails to understand what you say or who you are. Bear in mind that if you are not careful with how you spend your time, you will find out that this affects your spouse adversely, and she or he might start having issues that were not present in your marriage before this. Remember you are no longer alone, so plan your time with great care and consideration. Endeavour to plan accordingly and set aside your most valuable time for the person you love, rather than your friends!

Realize that, although spending time with friends without your spouse can be refreshing for most of you, as you are afforded a change of routine, note that this can be potentially dangerous for your marriage. The Bible tells us that couples must place a higher value on each other than they do on other relationships or as they may have done in the past. This means to consider what makes your spouse happy or sad so that while balancing your relationships like healthy friendships and hobbies go a long way to helping you feel good about yourself, remember in so doing, you must not forget that your spouse takes pre-eminence over every relationship you have. So, make time for your spouse or each other, be partner focused in other words, make your partner/ spouse a priority as you work toward a wholesome relationship characterized by love and respect and the fear of God. Do not let the fire go out of your relationship! Seize every opportunity to flirt with each other, joke and just be happy as you revel in one another. Do not be too serious and do your best to inject playfulness into your marriage.

Friendships should not be lopsided. Choose your friends with care so that each one of them contributes in some positive way to your life. You should not be the only one contributing to a relationship, or you will feel disgruntled and unhappy with the friendship. Friendships should operate on a give-and-take basis. Friendships are one of God's ways to enrich our lives. It is His way of putting good people in your life to make it better. However, some people may not really be your friends, and their presence can present various distracting and crippling effects on your life—especially if you're married.

I have watched and counselled couples engaged in worthless friendships who forgot that their dynamics and everything about their lives changes as soon as they say, "I do." When you get married, your friends and your interactions with your friends also change. There should be boundaries or, better, some measure of checks and balances. Your spouse is now your best friend, and you must accord her the respect a very intimate friend deserves. He/she now always comes first as both of you must work together to build your home and nurture your marriage and ditch friendships that could potentially cause problems. This, to some friends, might not sit well as they feel slighted and bitter at the change in your dynamics with them.

Some of your friends will become very toxic and hazardous to your marriage and can inadvertently break up your marriage if you are not careful. It is necessary to be wise and do away with these friendships. As with every relationship, you are better off without the added distractions.

Very early in my marriage, some friends were very toxic and had very bad habits. I think it is safe to say that all of us have had the "fair-weather friends," right? They could turn up like a bad penny. They were always around no matter what you did, they needed no invitation to invite themselves over and be around you 24/7. They were clingier and worse than the worst case of a flu virus. There was no thought of giving us a moment's privacy. They needed to portray themselves as very caring and loyal to "one spouse." On some occasions, they even fell asleep on the couches till the next day, and that meant you woke up catering to the sleepovers. Looking back, I think they felt it was some right they had been given to always be there. It was not all the friends we had who were this inconsiderate and toxic. Some became more like family members and knew how to maintain healthy boundaries and did not need to be told they could not be around all day. They knew their limits.

As a couple, we had little or no time to bond. At one stage, I felt I did not know my husband at all. This was because no day passed without their constant presence; we had little or no time as a couple to connect away from any distractions. I also felt very neglected as these friends were a constant feature in our plans. It was not long before we started having misunderstandings due to their incessant lies and rumour-mongering. They told these lies because it afforded them the opportunity to act as the "friend indeed." I could see they were very happy and had some sick pleasure in seeing us miserable. They found a way of just coming around early in the morning or after their lies to scout out their effect.

My husband could not see their deception and was so convinced that all their stories were true. He never believed or thought he should look deeper into these tales to unravel the truth. It was so difficult to make my husband see them for what they were, so I resigned myself to let sleeping dogs lie as I was tired of proving my innocence and explaining myself.

I took the matter to the Lord in prayer, as instructed in Philippians 4:6–7:

> Do not be anxious about anything, but in every situation, by prayer and petition, with thanksgiving, present your requests to God. And the peace of God, which transcends all understanding, will guard your hearts and your minds in Christ Jesus.

Need I tell you what peace I had after this? The Lord is really concerned about what affects us. His answers and rescue from these friends came most unexpectedly. I learned a very profound lesson while going through this: that I must always remember that even if I possessed some superpowers, I could not save these people from their pathological lies and wickedness. The power to do this was only theirs, and they had the choice of confessing their lies to the Lord and addressing this problem within themselves. In most cases, these people are very good at convincing you that what they are telling you is the truth when in fact it is the furthest thing from the truth.

I must confess that most times it is very difficult to see through their lies, but once you've identified your friend as a liar, it's important to distance yourself. My husband hung around these people because he felt a need to support them and carry them along. Unfortunately, while trying to do this, he constantly subjected us to their lies that were geared toward not only causing a rift in our relationship but bringing about a total breakup. These all happened because we had invested valuable time in people who had little or no intention of bringing positivity into our life; rather they saw our union as a threat to their friendship.

We have also had friends who shared little or no morals or religious ethics with us. Our intention was to bring them to the knowledge of the Lord. But all attempts failed as they had different ideas altogether. It is best to stay away from these people as it is not only vital but expedient for your friends to respect the fact that Jesus Christ is your Lord and Savior. If they do not share your faith or beliefs, you will be surrounded by people who do not share your views, and the danger here is that they will either convert you to their thinking or vice versa. Be careful to surround yourself with people who share your views because they are part of the world you are building and surrounding yourself with. The Bible enjoins us to choose wisely in Proverbs 27:17: "As iron sharpens iron, so one person sharpens another." I must tell you here that it was only by the grace of God that we could bridge all odds as a couple!

We wanted our marriage and lives to be a model of God's love to others, especially our non-believing friends. We reckoned we might be the only message or Bible these people might ever read or hear. If others could only see God's love in our marriage, they would naturally be curious! They would even want theirs to be like ours! We had to practice selfless love and devotion as these were in short supply and they were becoming rarer and rarer. We intended to be the exception! So, we allowed them to hang around us, hoping they would learn; thus seeds would be sown to the glory of the Lord. Some "converted" or believed for as long as it took them to achieve the motive of their friendship with us. However, keeping these people in tow meant we had zero to very few Christians who would build us up at that early start. As a result, we did not have faith believers who could provide us with positive mentorship or the dynamics to support our marriage. It was not hard to figure out that negative people could be a wedge within our marriage.

I think now, I can comfortably say I have lived through most types of friendships in marriage; however, another friend whom you do not want anywhere near you and would do better to cut out of your life is a close friend of the opposite sex. We all have them, but this type plays the trump card of being close to you and bites you in the process. They not only cause dissension, drama, and trouble but are capable of so much chaos in your life! These friends outwardly display "great care" and "consideration for your happiness," while inwardly are seething with a lot of envy. It leaves the spouse feeling threatened by this friend for one reason or another. It is a gut instinct that something is not right between the friends.

Most times, it has nothing to do with low self-esteem or some unresolved issue that took place in the past. It has to do with the fact that this friend wants more than to just be a friend. She/he wants it all. Why can he/she not have what you have? So, he positions himself as invaluable, very helpful, and harmless while all the time trying to be more! This friend ignores the other spouse or tries to show how intimate he/she is with the "friend." Conversations always revolve around how it was in the past, what they did, and end with "Oh, those days!" They are all contrived to make the other spouse feel left out or neglected.

This is where you draw the line and set boundaries between you and this friend. There is no better time as now to remember those vows you took to honour your spouse through sickness and in health—put that to work and honour the vows! The best way to do this is to have a talk with your friend and explain to her the issues her closeness is causing between you and your spouse. Make her understand that you are married to your spouse and there can be nothing between you two! You have chosen to be with your spouse and are happy with this choice and you wish her the best. If she wants to remain your friend, she will have to respect your spouse and the boundaries you have set. It would be better if you do not allow this friend to be part of your life, as you will find out that your marriage will always carry a third wheel that makes things uncomfortable, especially when she is around. This is because she will always make your wife feel she is lacking something and she can never be "good enough," even though she is the most important person in your life.

This passage in Mark 10:9, which instructs that "therefore what God has joined together, let no one separate" is one of the popular verses in the Bible. Most people know it and do not hesitate to reel it out when the need arises. How dearly do you hold the Word of the Lord? Some of you pick and choose the verses you want to hold onto and leave others that seem to speak directly to you. Others believe some were just meant for a set of people, so they do not apply to them. Well, the Bible tells us in Timothy 3:16 that "all Scripture is God-breathed and is useful for teaching, rebuking, correcting and training in righteousness." Contrary to our expectations, it is meant for all.

So, what do we make of this? Despite its popularity, do we know the implication of "let no one separate"? The "let no one separate" is not reflective of an outside force alone. It is also directed at the individual partners/spouses in the marriage. These vows speak of faithfulness toward one another, loyalty, trust, and selfless love. It is a love that is long-standing and abiding and will not faint at the slightest sign of problems. You can only separate from your spouse in cases where adultery has been committed or if you are involved in an extramarital affair or relationship. This notwithstanding is not supposed to be the first line of action. God wants you to work through all difficulties in marriage and stay united. The Bible says in Hebrews 13:4: "Marriage should be honored by all, and the marriage bed kept pure, for God will judge the adulterer and all the sexually immoral."

The marriage bed is to be kept pure and holy! There must be no blemish nor stain, and the Bible warns sternly against any sin in our sexual relations in marriage. Note here that when we commit any act that displeases the Lord, it is *sin*. We are enjoined to keep conjugal chastity and fidelity and to avoid all unseemly and immodest conduct with another person. We can commit adultery by being unchaste in thought as well as action. If, as married couples, you look at a woman or man and lust after her/him in your heart, even though nothing happens because you have not been sexually involved, you have committed adultery. Remember that nothing can be hidden from the sight of God as He knows what is going on in your heart and thoughts. When you introduce a third party of either sex into a marriage, it is automatically a violation of the very concept and precept of marriage.

One of the prerequisites of marriage is that we honour and worship God in our marriage through the love we have for our spouse. Most people feel very proud of themselves as they go about despising their marriage by indulging in extramarital affairs. They think they have gotten away with this sin as their wife or husband is not privy to their exploits. They exhibit a total disregard for their spouse and continue with their frolicking. Be cognizant of the fact that you may escape detection and judgment by your wife or your husband or the society or the state. But there is one who sees all, and He will surely judge, condemn, and punish this behaviour.

We must also understand that fornication and adultery are sins that defile us, as we see in Leviticus 18:20, where it is stated: "Do not have sexual relations with your neighbor's wife and defile yourself with her." A spouse can engage in such things and go back home, but he is forgetting a very important truth: he is bringing defilement to his marriage and his marriage bed. He has broken the command of keeping the marriage bed pure. Subsequently, he has defiled the marriage, even if such defilement is only of the transient thought about any other but his/her spouse. God places great value on the institution of marriage and wants all couples to honour it by obeying His commands and keeping the marriage holy and pure so that they can be blessed.

As a couple, you must strive to nurture these attributes in your marriage and be careful not to betray each other's trust as that would be the beginning of trouble in your lives. Bear in mind that trust is like a thread and once it is broken, even when tied back together, it leaves a knot and it is not very easy to work past that knot. This is the same with betrayed trust; it is difficult to reestablish as you will be living in fear of when next it will be betrayed again. However, with God, all things are possible. He will recreate in you a heart to love and trust again.

As a couple, you must determine to work toward building a happy, harmonious, lifelong marriage. As I stated earlier, may I again take this opportunity to remind you that marriage is not a "once and for all living happily ever after." It's an everyday commitment/a covenant for life for both spouses. If you do not commit to working hard toward achieving your goal of marital bliss, the devil will be all too happy to assist you in dissolving it. In line with this, the Bible cautions in 1 Peter 5:8–9 that we must:

> Be alert and of sober mind. Your enemy the devil prowls around like a roaring lion looking for someone to devour. Resist him, standing firm in the faith, because you know that the family of believers throughout the world is undergoing the same kind of sufferings.

It is not very surprising that when we look at the things men need from a relationship, we find respect mentioned as one of them. The Bible tells us in Romans 12:10 to "be devoted to one another in love. Honor one another above yourselves." It is often the case that we might ask, how do we show or display honour? This is done through something as simple as the way we speak to each other or about each other in the other person's absence. This can also be seen in our behaviour and our conduct in and outside the home. It is showing respect that says, "I do not only claim to love you but hold you in the highest esteem." This love must be honest without guile, hypocrisy, arrogance, or pretense. It must be understood that when we disagree and fail to make up, it shows that our hearts are not right with God and our spouse.

This reveals our selfishness and pride as we are elevating ourselves above others and being inconsiderate. This is what the Bible says in 1 Peter 3:7:

> Husbands, in the same way be
> considerate as you live with your
> wives, and treat them with respect as
> the weaker partner and as heirs with
> you of the gracious gift of life, so that
> nothing will hinder your prayer.

If translated directly, your prayers will be hindered, and you will wonder why. We must note that often answers to prayers are dependent on a man's treatment of his wife. We don't expect to dishonour God's gift and still receive His nod of approval concerning some other aspects. You are dishonouring God if you cannot find it in you as husbands to be considerate and respectful toward your wives. Note that God is a very just God and does not work in confusion.

In all our lives, we must emulate Jesus as He, being God, humbled Himself for us by becoming a servant and dying on the cross for our sins. This should tell us that it is foolish for any man to put himself above his spouse or others, as there will be no joy or happiness in his life. Our lives, therefore, must be reflective of what Christ has done for us and called us to. I am going to use the New Living Translation Bible quote here for emphasis because I love the way it puts this across. Ephesians 4:2–3 says:

> Always be humble and gentle. Be patient
> with each other, making allowance for
> each other's faults because of your love.

> Make every effort to keep yourselves
> united in the Spirit, binding yourselves
> together with peace.

Put simply, we are being told here that our unity with our spouse comes from within, and it is because of the spirit of God working within us.

As a couple, pride and arrogance should have no place in your lives. It has always been the case that couples are never willing to humble themselves and work in love and unity. They have elevated themselves above each other and are ready to act as both the jury and the judge in the home, ready to believe the worst of the other rather than admit they are wrong. They consistently push or force their opinions on others, even when they are very wrong in their thinking or belief. Some of you thrive on the path of making your spouse feel small while you feel like a king. Well, there is nothing like this when you are a follower of Christ.

With behaviour like this, how can you strive to be patient with each other? Do not forget that part of the Scripture we are discussing enjoins us to "be patient bearing with one another in love." It is necessary to understand that trying to build anything that is not built on Christian or biblical tenets is like building on a rocky foundation. It is easier to practice patience with one another when you are aware of what is required of you as the Spirit of God will help you realize your individual differences. He will give you the grace you need to bear with each other in love. This is most important because marriage, as stated before, is between two different people who have decided to make a home together. In this process, they strive to understand each other and build a fulfilling and long-lasting marriage.

We might pretend that we do not know what is happening to us Christians today. We try to do everything on our own power and have put very little effort into our marriages. This has resulted in us getting nothing or very little out of this wonderful institution. We read the Bible and learn of the need to apply God's love toward our brothers and sisters in the Lord. We try to apply this principle to others and carry other's burdens, praying even for the lost. What is ironic, therefore, is that we fail woefully when it comes to our spouse as nothing whatsoever actually brings about a change in our behaviour toward each other. The truth here is that God's kind of love must be applied to our marriage too. After all, charity begins at home.

We must live in peace and unity with one another. This is just saying that even in your disagreements, find ways to communicate with each other so that you are not disagreeing with who they are but with their position or viewpoint. Work consciously together to resolve all issues amicably without hurting each other, and make your marriage blessed and fulfilled. Be careful not to strip each other of the power or right to contribute toward decision-making. You have not been given the right by God to lord it over your spouse. I am saying this because a friend of mine could not make decisions or contribute to making them as her husband felt she lacked the wisdom to do so. This, however, was not true as she was well-educated and of sound mind. She became very timid and could not see herself as capable of doing anything.

My point here is that you should take the time to invest in each other. Talk about everything and never belittle another's input. Strive to live according to the calling we have in Christ Jesus. Be mindful of the fact that both of you have been assigned very significant and different roles in the family and in the church. This in no way makes one of you more superior than the other. The husband is the husband—the leader, protector, and guide to his family members—and the wife is the wife—the helper, co-heir, and not a slave to a master!

Even when God comes down physically and handpicks you a spouse, He never promises that you will never have problems. He has just given you a spouse He has designed with you in mind, who will complement your attributes. He just wants us to know that He will never leave nor forsake us, so all we need to do is do our work, to turn to Him in our times of need and just surrender everything to Him. By the mere fact that we live on Earth, we must be cognizant of the fact that we will go through trials, but in Jesus, we will not find it difficult to solve these problems.

Problems will arise especially if we don't involve the Maker in our marriage or union.

As a couple, you must determine that you are in this together: the investments, the ups and downs you face, and the several blessings our Lord has bestowed upon you as a couple/family are a great source for thankfulness! Developing and maintaining a healthy marriage requires a lot of hard work and sacrifice. Commit it to the Lord and He will guide you.

Do not be anxious about anything, but in every situation, by prayer and petition, with thanksgiving, present your requests to God. And the peace of God, which transcends all understanding, will guard your hearts and your minds in Christ Jesus.

Finally, brothers and sisters, whatever is true, whatever is noble, whatever is right, whatever is pure, whatever is lovely, whatever is admirable—if anything is excellent or praiseworthy— think about such things.

—Philippians 4:6–8

Chapter Fifteen

Embracing Change

Sometimes when you go through a particular phase in your life, I am sure you wish it were possible for life to just remain the same, with no changes and no challenges at all. You can wish all your life and still see and experience change. Change is a constant in life. In most cases, it is not something we love as some changes can really make us feel overwhelmed and distraught. Change in life is inevitable as circumstances we are exposed to change us.

Everything surrounding us—life, time, ideas, and even technological advances—changes us. This does not make change feel any better as with every change, we feel as if everything we knew or held dear is slipping out of our hands. This makes us feel betrayed, especially when we suspect that our spouse is changing faster than we anticipated or can even comprehend. We see this as them growing up into someone different from the sweetheart we married and vowed to love unconditionally.

An unending list of ongoing changes can occur in our lives. After conception, we undergo a series of changes as we change from an embryo, then a fetus, then an infant, a toddler, a small child, preteen, teen, young adult, and so on. Our brains change, our bodies change, our knowledge base changes, our skill base changes, our likes and dislikes change, and our habits change. Everything changes as we embrace life and reach our optimal potential.

As human beings, we all are on the path of change, and we will continue to evolve to better versions of ourselves throughout our lives. The best part about this is that change is different and unique for each one of us, and it can happen independently of someone else. A woman undergoes the greatest change when she enters a marriage. Before marriage, she is a daughter, a friend, and a sister in her family. However, after marriage, her roles change almost overnight. She realizes suddenly that she must be a wife, a daughter-in-law, and in the future a mother too, while still being a daughter and a sister. She has left behind her usual routine of life and her parents' home to be with the man she loves after the wedding. Therefore, a woman has to experience a lot of changes after marriage, which can be both enriching and daunting at the same time. These changes are not in any way meant to break her but to mould her into what God has made her to be. She has to fulfill all the roles ahead of her with great aplomb. This is where she can confidently cast her burdens on the Lord so He can help her through life.

During our marriage, we go through a series of changes so that on introspection, we realize that we are not the same as we were before our wedding day, so it should not come as a surprise to us that our spouse will not be the same as when we married or grow old with, and neither will we. A lot of factors like age, wisdom, maturity, life experiences, and so on contribute to this change and make them better.

I advise you to look back on your life; you will notice immediately that you are much older than you were before your marriage, more matured too. You will also be able to see and, if possible, relive different chapters of your life as they begin to unfold. Apart from the attributes I have mentioned, you can also likely see how you are not quite the same person you were back then. I am not trying to say you are so different that your personality has changed. The truth is that the things you held dear might seem lame to you at this stage. Even your outlook on life might be different. Your priorities have shifted. Your motivations are different.

When I look back on my life, I am forced to accept that I needed this change to survive a lot of the challenges we have been exposed to as a married couple with five children. I have also come to realize that my relationship with my spouse needed this transformational change as it brought us closer to

God and each other. It also made us stronger and better able to handle our problems and work together as a team. It has been a blessing to submit wholly to the lordship of the Father as we went through these changes. Even though this change had to be embraced naturally most of the time, I am not in any way trying to say I have always appreciated and loved change as some changes meant a lot. You will barely be able to comprehend how some of these changes happened even though they were in your best interest.

Like Abram, in Genesis 12:1–3, the call of Abram, the Bible says:

> The LORD had said to Abram, "Go from your country, your people and your father's household to the land I will show you. I will make you into a great nation, and I will bless you; I will make your name great, and you will be a blessing. I will bless those who bless you and whoever curses you I will curse; and all peoples on earth will be blessed through you."

By writing this, I am not trying to compare myself to Abram in any way. This is to express how I felt at leaving my familiar environment and going to a foreign and unknown land. We had to pack up and leave all family behind to go to an unfamiliar land and start our lives there. My husband had gone months before me, and I now had to do this on my own with three little children all under three! The scariest part was not travelling alone with three kids but the thought of starting all over again. We had left our comfort zone where we had everything— family, friends, jobs, help with the children, and above all the knowledge and safety of everything familiar. What this meant was that we also left all our material possessions behind as we could not travel with these abroad. So, it meant a clean start. With God as my guide, I made the journey with my three little children to meet my husband. It was a total shock to finally arrive and understand that it was not going to be the same. I did not have siblings, a mother, or a father to run to for some wise tips.

My first intention was not to look for new friends but to hold on very tightly to my God—so tightly that He became my present help in a time of need as stated in the King James Version, specifically in Psalm 46:1–11:

> God is our refuge and strength, a very
> present help in trouble. Therefore we
> will not fear, though the earth be
> removed, and though the mountains
> be carried into the midst of the sea;
> Though the waters thereof roar and
> be troubled, though the mountains
> shake with the swelling thereof. Selah.
> There is a river, the streams whereof

shall make glad the city of God, the holy place of the tabernacles of the most High. God is in the midst of her; she shall not be moved: God shall help her, and that right early. The heathen raged, the kingdoms were moved: he uttered his voice, the earth melted. The LORD of hosts is with us; the God of Jacob is our refuge. Selah. Come, behold the works of the LORD, what desolations he hath made in the earth. He maketh wars to cease unto the end of the earth; he breaketh the bow, and cutteth the spear in sunder; he burneth the chariot in the fire. Be still, and know that I am God: I will be exalted among the heathen, I will be exalted in the earth. The LORD of hosts is with us; the God of Jacob is our refuge. Selah.

Make no mistake here. Although this change was for a better opportunity, it was not considered nice by me. Hello, I was uprooted from all I was comfortable in. But as I look back, I realize if we had not done that we would not be where we are today. We underwent what I call "a total attitudinal transformation." We came to the knowledge that we were all alone and became solely dependent on the Lord who had taken us there. My husband and I held onto each other and became best friends, confidants, and above all, husband and wife and parents to our three children, soon to be four. Loving God and serving Him and being with one another became very big priorities in our lives as we raised our family. Our focus on God helped us tremendously to go through this phase of our lives.

Experiencing this change so early in life made us realize the value of being friends with your spouse. Without this, being in a very strange place with little children, not able to speak the language, and trying to find our footing would have been very impossible. Our growth started from here with the understanding that we had God and each other to run to. This helped us through the stressful period of the change. Having a confidant made it all worthwhile.

As we began this journey, my husband and I embraced change and changed together. We left home as two pampered young adults and matured after we moved because we stayed side by side in everything. All choices were made in agreement, after communicating with each other and placing them in prayer before the Lord God. The importance of Matthew 18:19–20, which states, "Again, truly I tell you that if two of you on earth agree about anything they ask for, it will be done for them by my Father in heaven. For where two or three gather in my name, there am I with them," became a reality in our lives. Instead of spending time wallowing in self-pity and loneliness, while resisting and criticizing each other, we embraced it as a sign of growth and life. Instead of approaching change with fear or regarding it as a sign of betrayal, we knew that God had a valid plan for taking us out of the familiar to the unknown, and as a result, my husband and I were not stagnated but became ever-evolving beings with unlimited potential for transformation as we trod this path.

We immediately understood that just as with everything in life, marriage too undergoes changes. As there are seasons for everything on the earth, marriage has its seasons. It changes because it is a very dynamic relationship that exists between two people. As we grow older each day, we embrace life and change occurs in our lives. We need to be ready for this and be willing to adapt to it as part of our lives, and if this does not happen, we start feeling oppressed by change or lack of change. If we are in a long-term relationship, each partner is likely to evolve from the person we fell in love with into someone new—and they do not need to evolve into someone spectacular, well-rounded, smarter, or more fun.

Personal change and growth can become issues in marriage because we are all created uniquely different and develop at different rates. We have expectations, and we want and hope our spouses will change any bad habits or dysfunction for the better. However, we are all works-in-progress. When we embark upon the journey of change, we want it to happen immediately, but sometimes it doesn't happen fast enough to suit us. Our spouse may be oblivious to our dissatisfaction or discontentment. Most of us do not realize the need to change something no matter how glaring it is, but a loving spouse can gently ask for change. It is important to try and avoid nagging, manipulation, cajoling, and arguing, as this will get us nowhere and can make us even more miserable.

We must understand that for a successful marriage, there is a need for us to recognize that change starts from us—the only person we can change is ourself. As the saying goes, "You cannot teach an old dog new tricks." If possible, enlist your spouse as your partner in self-change. It is necessary that when you have resolved and are willing to change some behaviour, let your spouse know about your plan to change and enlist their support. This will ignite a renewed respect and marital growth between both partners in the marriage.

Realize that change is most often an indication of growth. It indicates that you are growing as God intended. So, as couples, you must give your spouse permission to change to allow them to grow, evolve, or progress. It is common knowledge that not all change is positive or healthy change; however, when you take this as part of life, it will become easier for all involved. This change might not come with all you anticipated or wished for, but be thankful that because of change, you are not the same as you were when you got married. I am personally grateful for change as it has brought about a lot of differences in our lives. No longer are we so inexperienced and naive as we were before.

As a couple, encourage your spouse to work and embrace change so that they can evolve into the man or woman they were meant to be and choose to be. Never try to shape their behaviour or personality to suit you, as this will only end up in frustration, conflict, and a strained relationship. Trying to impose your wishes on your spouse will make them feel small and unappreciated. They will not be able to be themselves, especially in the presence of others.

I remember a very old friend who never wanted to go out with her husband because he always tried to correct her in the presence of others. She confessed that she could never relax and be herself as he made her feel very embarrassed simply because she tried to be her real self in the presence of others. He felt she was too "friendly with his friends." As a result, she believed she was not good enough and felt rejected by her spouse. Whenever he invited her out, she became very anxious and feigned a headache. I remember her asking once what we thought of her as a person. She buried the resentment she felt toward her husband and started displaying symptoms of anxiety and depression, feelings of sadness, anger, resentment, and possible thoughts of infidelity. All she wanted was for her husband to respect her as the Bible directs and to not make her feel embarrassed by who she was or what she was not.

The thought of change should not become so consuming that it steals the peace away from your marriage. Your spouse, no matter what personal faults or issues they may have, will appreciate your efforts. Most times in your quest for change, you become frustrated if your operation-change strategy doesn't light a fire under your spouse. Despite your hopes and personal improvement efforts, he or she may be resistant or unable to change as you may like. You do not need to be disappointed or feel bewildered. You can just work toward your own self-change and gradually get to acceptance.

When spouses show each other love and acceptance, they respond more quickly to each other's changes. Be ready to support any effort your spouse makes toward change, no matter how tentative or incomplete that effort is. If he or she discloses a desire to change, be ready to help and not hinder the process. It may be that professional help is in order, but your role as helpmate is indispensable. You are the one who loves and knows your spouse the most. May I enjoin you here that if you want to have a fulfilled relationship, skip the comparison game with your friends.

Experience has taught me that most of the stories traded between friends are probably false and wishful thinking. I would say to be careful of the friend who always has an answer to a question or has been through a similar situation. Sometimes he has a friend who has a friend who has gone through a situation you have just experienced or described. He appears quick-witted and very knowledgeable! If you are not careful, you will find out to your surprise that you have destroyed your marriage because you could not decipher between falsehood and truth. Soon enough, you become like him or even worse than he is.

It would not be surprising if your lovey-dovey spouse who could not wait to get under the sheets with you suddenly becomes too sleep-obsessed and too tired. The normal feeling spouses experience at such time is that of betrayal and outrage by this change. After all, they fell in love with one person, and they are now faced with someone who doesn't seem familiar anymore. They decide he or she violated the marriage contract. You feel very resentful toward this change. The natural impulse here is to try to kick against this perceived difference, which is "change."

You forget that being happy and contented with a spouse or yourself requires that you must find ways to be happy with different versions of that person. You must choose to purposely be happy. This is the only solution because how can you give happiness when you do not feel or have not experienced it? Let us be real here—you cannot give what you do not have!

Whatever you do, do not forget to respect, care, and understand each other's viewpoint as you embrace change. So, strive to honour each other so that your prayers as a couple may not be hindered. Trust in the Lord and each other. Be courageous enough to stand up for the truth and to do what is right and work in complete understanding that no matter the storm you go through in life, Christ will be there with you and He will see you through. Never lose your self-confidence and hope in the Lord as this is what will see you through every change and trial you encounter. Be completely honest with one another.

A Quick Note

As you work toward fulfillment and love in your marriage, consider the following questions:

- Is God at the head of your marriage? Look closely and see what drives your marriage.
- Have you and your spouse achieved your desired unity?
- Do you recognize and know your common goals?
- Are you living in harmony or in competition with each other?
- Have you as a couple really cleaved together and left others out?
- Are you completely honest with one another?
- Is your marriage a stable basis from where all other relationships arise?
- As parents, are you determined to share equal responsibility for raising children and training them in the way of the Lord?
- Is the husband fulfilling the protective role assigned to him by God?

Meditate upon Philippians 4:8:

> Finally, brothers and sisters, whatever is true, whatever is noble, whatever is right, whatever is pure, whatever is lovely, whatever is admirable—if anything is excellent or praiseworthy—think about such things.

Summary

A must-have for all couples, newlyweds, those long in love, and engaged. This book is a crash course on married life, from how to argue like adults to making financial plans for the future, and above all, how to get along with your in-laws! Written from a faith perspective with biblical backing and real-life anecdotes, *My Spouse, My Friend* is your guide to navigating questions about married life and finding those answers that you really need.

Note: All texts used in this book are taken from the Holy Bible with particular reference to the New International Version unless otherwise stated.

Bio

Ingiete Oyama is a married, accomplished and well-educated woman whose passions lean heavily toward helping others. She has a degree in counselling and master's degrees in, child and adolescent welfare, occupational health, and rehabilitation and return to work, as well as other credits in addiction and behaviour management. She enjoys cooking without recipes, reading a wide array of novels, and giving unsolicited advice to her five children.

Made in the USA
Monee, IL
24 June 2021